THE DELUGE

THE DELUGE

New Vietnamese Poetry

edited and translated by

Linh Dinh

with an introduction by

Hai-Dang Phan

chax press 2013

tucson arizona

ISBN 978-0-9894316-3-7

Published by Chax Press in 2013

Chax Press
411 N 7th Ave Ste 103
Tucson, Arizona 85705-8388

Contents

What's New in Vietnamese Poetry
Linh Dinh Interviews Phan Nhien Hao
Introducing Ly Doi and Bui Chat

Introduction

he became lost and found himself in the deluge
— Nguyen Quoc Chanh

1/

In the audio clip I am listening to of Nguyen Quoc Chanh reading his poetry you can actually hear the sounds of a city: the drone of motorbikes gliding down avenues, stray horn beeps of taxis angling through congestion, an emphatic voice from the crowd rising and breaking like a lone cloud. To my ears, it sounds just like Ho Chi Minh City. Audible about mid-way into the third-line of the first poem in Chanh's samizdat *Hey, I'm Here* (2005), what we hear is not the product of a sound-proof studio, but a porous echo-chamber for the improvisation of the "Disconnected Thoughts" in the title of Chanh's poem:

> Saigon punctured, a corpse not yet buried, the capital sinks a few inches each day [...] words survive thanks to crossbreeding [...] A national secret is the feasts derived from the fortunes of poppies, to be human is to be humiliated, to be Vietnamese is to be super humiliated [...] Someone advertises on the Web: I need a sexual partner who's a vanguard in thoughts and actions...."

Chanh leaves in what other poets edit out, neither censoring the contradictions of the self nor the offenses of the world. His poems get us closer to the temperature on the street—its accidental encounters and collisions, aleatory noise, liquid language, quick commerce and quicker corruption, refuse and wreckage. Accidentally recorded or not, the urban soundscape offers a fitting accompaniment to the words flowing from the poet's mouth and helps capture something of the atmosphere conditions of *The Deluge*, an anthology of new Vietnamese poetry. Read in a room somewhere in Ho Chi Minh City, uploaded and e-mailed to the Berlin-based webzine *talawas*, and downloaded to my computer as an audio file, I listen to the voice streaming into my room in Gainesville, Florida. I imagine Chanh—but it could be any of the poets in this anthology really—reading aloud to an imagined audience scattered throughout the city and dispersed across the globe, each word an affirmation and reminder of the poet to his republic: "Hey, I'm Here"—and I'm not going away.

A rebellious spirit dwells throughout the poets and poetry in this anthology. You just heard it in Nguyen Quoc Chanh. You hear it in the opening poem of the anthology, "Resurrection," when Thanh Tam Tuyen calls out his own name amidst desolation—"I want to cry like I want to vomit / on the street / crystal sunlight / I call my own name to soothe my longing." You see it in the depictions of social and psychic devastation in the war poems of Tran Da Tu and also in the portraits of individual and collective disillusionment in the postwar poems of Trang Vang Sao. You feel it in the liberating confluence of different poetic traditions in Phan Nhien Hao's poetry. You can smell it too in the foul, "Open Mouth" poetries of Bui Chat, Ly Doi, and Lyn Bacardi. In their individual ways, the [twenty six] poets here refuse to do and say what's deemed acceptable, whether it's about the body or society they live in, the literary traditions and cultural histories they inherit, or the present tense they inhabit. These unruly ways involve the new forms of thought and feeling experimented with in their poetry: from the mercurial temperament of the prose poem to the concentration of the short lyric, from the disorienting imagery of surrealism to the detailed depictions of social realism, from the live wire of everyday speech to the synapse firings of ordinary consciousness. Gathered together for the first time, they share a language, a genre, and a complex history. Measured in syllables, syntax, and tonal shifts, the new Vietnamese poetry is a barometer to the turbulent changes in the cultural and literary climate in Vietnam during the later half of the twentieth century as well as to the global transformations of the early twenty-first. This anthology consists of poets living and writing in Vietnam and nearly an equal number overseas in countries other than Vietnam. Also, nearly half represent the generation who witnessed the war in Vietnam as either civilians or combatants and the other half the generation who either grew up or were born in the wake of war. However it's divided, this anthology offers a unique sampling of past and present voices at the vanguard of Vietnamese poetry worldwide, a long awaited and necessary *deluge* of dissident, diasporic, and defiant voices.

2 /

Til other voices wake
us or we drown
—George Oppen

You won't find many of the poets collected in this anthology in
bookstores in Vietnam. But for anyone familiar with the nature of writing
and publishing in Vietnam—where independent presses and journals are
nonexistent, public poetry readings are broken up, Vietnamese literature written
overseas unacknowledged or derided, and where you can write whatever you
want so long as you avoid politics—this should come as little surprise.

On a recent trip back to Vietnam, I combed through the Poetry and
Literature sections of all of the bookstores I visited in Ho Chi Minh City and
Da Nang, making mental notes of who and what was on the shelves. In every
bookstore, big or small, new or used, you can find these slim, pocket-size
editions of selected poems by popular poets such as: Tan Da, The Lu, Han Mac
Tu, Xuan Dieu, Nguyen Binh, Xuan Quynh, Te Hanh, Luu Trong Lu, Ho Dzenh,
Vu Hoang Chuong. Also readily available were shiny, attractively repackaged
editions of a number of revolutionary poets such as To Huu, Xuan Dieu, and
Che Lan Vien, each buttressed by literary biographies and criticism. For the
few high school and college students studying literature, there were affordable,
critical editions of modern Vietnamese poets and poetry.

More interestingly, I found reprint editions of *Vietnamese Poets,*
1932-1941, Hoai Thanh's groundbreaking anthology of influential poets of
the 1930's. Published in 1942, with critical introductions and annotations by
Hoai Thanh, the anthology showcases a number of poets associated with the
Tho Moi or "New Poetry" movement, including Xuan Dieu, Luu Trong Lu,
Huy Can, The Lu, and Che Lan Vien. Influenced by the French Romanticists
and Symbolists taught in colonial schools and available in translation, spurred
by the Romanized, national script of *quoc ngu* coming into widespread use,
and adapting Western ideas for the modernization of Vietnamese culture
and society, these and other poets began departing from the poetic forms
and traditions inherited from China. No longer bound strictly to the values
of Confucian society, the "New Poetry" turned inward to express, in lyrics of
gentle rhythms and memorable lines, individual experiences of love, suffering,
and loss. Popular and readable, this was the kind of poetry young Vietnamese
would commit to memory, copy down into private notebooks, or set to music.
By the August Revolution of 1945, however many poets formerly associated
with the "New Poetry" movement, Xuan Dieu and Che Lan Vien most notably
among them, rejected their so-called reactionary, decadent, and bourgeois

poetic selves, and embraced the cause of revolutionary struggle by taking up the new standard of socialist realism.

Not everyone marched in lock-step. Harder to find were poets belonging to the infamous and influential *Nhan Van Giai Pham*, an outspoken group of artists and intellectuals active in the North during the 1950's. They demanded greater political and creative freedoms, and critiqued the abuses of the Vietnamese Communist Party. In one particularly good used bookstore, I discovered beaten-up copies of the three-volume collected poetry and prose of Hoang Cam, a key member of *Nhan Van Giai Pham*. In March of 2007, Hoang Cam was one of four poets associated with the dissident group—the other three being Le Dat, Phung Quan, and Tran Dan—awarded Vietnam's highest literary prize, fifty years after they were tried, imprisoned and silenced by the Party for the oppositional politics expressed in their poetry and prose.

Of the contemporary poetry represented, I only saw a few stray copies of collections by Nguyen Duy, Huu Tinh, and Nguyen Quang Thieu. As for translations, I was thrilled to find a copy of a selection of Brecht's poetry in Vietnamese, its English counterpart virtually impossible to find in the States. In the same bookstore in Da Nang where I found the collected works of Hoang Cam, I chanced upon a copy of Nguyen Huu Hong Minh's book *Giong noi mo ho* on the discount shelf, but found no other books by poets in this anthology who I knew had once published collections in Vietnam. There was hardly a trace of the once flourishing poetic culture of South Vietnam before 1975, save one strange exception. Nearly every bookstore carried copies of reissued editions of poetry by Bui Giang, known for his vagrant life, unconventional poems, and copious translations. He was perhaps the closest thing Vietnam has ever produced to a beatnik poet. My father, long an admirer of Bui Giang's poetry, shrugged off the revival as a literary fad. Still, he scooped up a handful of copies to add to his private library at home.

3 /

a shout is a prayer
for the waiting centuries
— Thanh Tam Tuyen

The Fall of Saigon, The Liberation of the South, The Reunification of Vietnam—for different people the date, April 30, 1975, conjures different things. For many writers of former South Vietnam, it evokes not just the fall of a country but also the fall of a literature. Saigon would be officially renamed Ho Chi Minh City, its boulevards, avenues, and streets also renamed to commemorate revolutionary figures, events, and slogans. So too Vietnamese literary history would be eventually dismantled, systematically re-written or outright erased; books would be banned, confiscated, and burned; writers silenced, censored, and imprisoned. Writer and critic Vo Phien "recall[s] that Monday, May 26, 1975 in a refugee camp on Guam. Just up in the morning, we heard on the radio that it had become illegal in Vietnam to sell reading matter published under the old regime and that as of the previous Thursday, all Saigon bookshops had been closed down. We, writer-refugees shook our heads: we had only made it half way to our new land and at home our books had already found their final moments."

Part recovery project, this anthology attempts to revive a number of important poets writing in former South Vietnam during the 1960's and 70's. They are part of a lost generation, whose works have all but literally vanished in Vietnam, where official versions of the national literature erase the literary heritage of the South between 1954-1975, and are virtually invisible to readers in the U.S., where literature written in languages other than English drift into the blind-spot of a literary culture still driven by a monolingual approach to a multilingual reality.

The anthology appropriately begins with Thanh Tam Tuyen, one of the most influential poets writing in South Vietnam before 1975. In 1956, he helped establish the influential literary journal *Sang Tao* or *Creativity*. A central figure in a Saigon literary scene bustling with artistic and intellectual energy, he called upon poets to abandon the rhyming forms and romantic content that dominated the literary landscape and resist as well the injunction for poetry to serve politics. Instead, he theorized and experimented with a form of "free verse" in which what he referred to as the "rhythm of images" and the "rhythm of thoughts" combined to form the "expressions of the rhythm of consciousness," as electrifyingly realized in what is perhaps his most famous poem, "Resurrection":

I want to live like I want to die
among intersecting breaths
a flaming chest
I call softly
dear
open the door to your heart
my living spirit has turned into a child
as pure as the truth one time.

Clean, stark, and spare, not a syllable wasted here. Though his poems may cry of urban alienation, which they certainly do, their song is also pitched in exalted and ecstatic tones. In this poem and elsewhere, his sources of creative influence and inspiration include Existentialist philosophy, Buddhism, French Surrealism, and American jazz. His brilliance is to channel these alternating currents towards the creation of singular, jolting, often prophetic forms of perception and consciousness. "In the name of / Love freedom man," which are his true poetic trinity, Tuyen attains a fullness and plentitude of rare poetic vision.

Like many of the poets in this anthology, Tuyen was both a participant and witness to the war. He served two stints in the Army Republic of Vietnam, first from 1962 to 1966, then from 1968 until the end of the war in 1975. In "Three-Quarter Time," he addresses a fallen friend: "A round bullet hole on your chest / A bayonet through the lung / Heart still beating / In three-quarter time." On the other side of the fighting, Tran Vang Sao and Thanh Thao both dispatched deeply skeptical poetry on the brutality and sorrow of war. Thanh Thao, who worked for Vietnamese Army Radio of the North, became well known for his long poem about the travails of war, "A Soldier Speaks of His Generation." Tran Vang Sao joined the National Liberation Front in 1965. The specter of war continues to haunt his poems of the 1980's and 1990's. In his poem of the same title, a single "Night" in 1990 becomes the reservoir for an endless catalogue of individual and collective trauma:

1975

night of demonstrations on the streets
tanks hand grenades concertina barb wires
masks and hunting dogs

night during war staying up to watch a corpse
night of B52 vomiting chemicals

night in 1968
night of espionage

Some of the most powerful and original poetic responses to the war, in either Vietnamese or English, belong to Tran Da Tu. Poems such as, "Love Tokens," "Toy for Future Children," and "Fragmented War," all written during the mid-1960s, ought to be considered as vital contributions to the unfortunately vast archive of twentieth-century poetry of witness. In "Love Tokens," Tu draws on the conceits of conventional love poetry to speak to the aftermath of war:

> I'll give you a car bomb
> A car bomb exploding on a crowded street
> On a crowded street exploding flesh and bones
> That's our festival, don't you understand
>
> I'll give you a savage war

There's an explosive, jarring effect to Tu's dilatory lines, masterfully captured in Dinh's translation, and all the more haunting for the way they reverberate into our present war zones. Overall, the result is a striking assessment of the social ruin war bestows onto the future, as figured quite literally in "Toy for Future Children," a poem which invokes the voice and tone of children's tales ("A blind and deaf bullet buried in the field / Dozing through decades of blood and bones / Then one morning / In a bustling future / As the children return to the field") in an apology for the moral failings of parents, the buried legacy of war they leave behind. Written by a dissident poet who lived in the South during the war, where much of the bloodiest fighting took place, Tu's poetry documents the human cost of that inhumane war from a perspective too often neglected in Vietnam and the U.S. and with an arresting style seldom seen anywhere.

Poets like Thanh Tam Tuyen and Tran Da Tu represent just two entries in the archive of poetry of South Vietnam that remain submerged by literary forgetfulness. A first attempt, this anthology hopes to create an opening for a chorus of other poets from Vietnam still waiting to be heard: Bui Giang, Mai Thao, Nha Ca, Nguyen Bac Son, Nguyen Duc Son, To Thuy Yen, Vu Hoang Chuong.

4 /

You who will emerge from the flood
In which we have gone under
Remember
When you speak of our failings
The dark time too
Which you have escaped
—Bertolt Brecht

Translated into Vietnamese, Brecht's "To Those Born Later" finds an especially appropriate addressee in the postwar generation of Vietnamese poets. After 1975, Vietnam emerged from the dark time of war only to plunge into the outer dark of peacetime: wars in Cambodia and against the Chinese, policy-driven poverty and foot shortages, an already stagnant economy further strangled by a U.S. trade embargo, scores of its citizenry thrown into "re-education" camps, widespread corruption among party officials, waves of its population pouring overseas. Almost half of the poets gathered here either grew up or were born during this prolonged aftermath: Nguyen Quoc Chanh (b. 1958), Phan Nhien Hao (b. 1967), Nguyen Huu Hong Minh (b. 1971), Phan Huyen Thu (b. 1972), Van Cam Hai (b. 1972), Phan Ba Tho (b. 1972), Mien Dang (b. 1974). Ai Van Quoc (b. 1975), Hoang Da Thi (b. 1978), Ly Doi (b. 1978), Bui Chat (b. 1979), and Lynh Bacardi (b. 1981).

Judging from the poems in this anthology, the sensory organs of this postwar generation of poets evolved to survive the times, the light meter of their poetic vision recalibrated to different tonalities of dark. This would at least partly explain the prevalence of night and its boundary blurring logic in so many of their poems: night sets the rhythm for the improvisation of thought and feeling in Phan Nhien Hao's surreal and soulful quartet of poems on the melancholy of exile ("Night Freedom," "Night's Dawn," "Night, Fish and Charlie Parker," and "Night in the South"); "Night slithers slowly into the Perfume River" of Phan Huyen Thu's stately flowing, de-romanticized vision of modern day prostitutes plying their trade in the ancient capital of Hue; "the flow of night is level" in the hallucinatory, verbal vortex of Van Cam Hai's poems such as "Deluge," where "the head of the storm surges forward searching for a prey / an urban nest / street intersections spill out." For all of these poets, as Thanh Thao writes in his millennial reflection "Slow Passage 2000," "those who seek in night / a task a hope a place of refuge a void / the night promises everything."

Hoang Da Thi was the first of the postwar generation of poets to be born after 1975. Hoang's playful and precocious poems were spoken by her when she was between the ages of 3 and 5, and recorded by her mother, the well-known poet Lam Thi My Da. Here's all four lines of the poem "Star Buttons": "The sky is like a roof / The sky is like a shirt / A shirt has many buttons / Those are star buttons." Simple, silly, and even a little surreal in its syllogistic construction, the poem brims with childhood innocence and imagination. Compare the daughter's picture of the sky with her mother's war-time commemoration of the death of a female comrade in the poem "A Sky in a Bomb Crater"—"I gazed into the center of the crater / where you'd died and saw the sky in the pool / of rain water. Our country is so kind: / water from the sky washes the pain away"—and you begin to see how the daughter's childhood poetry expresses the spirit of rebirth and renewal of a nation eager to leave its painful past behind: a *tabula rasa*, absent of any reference to death and destruction.

As someone also born after 1975, whose parents and immediate family experienced the war in Vietnam as combatants and civilians, I wonder what Hoang Da Thi's poems written in adulthood look like, whether and how she inherited her mother's dark skies. The predicament of the second generation, writes Eva Hoffman, is that we inherit "not experience, but its shadows." And shadows, everyone knows, possess an uncanny familiarity and strangeness, intimacy and distance. In the spoken and unspoken idiom of familial communication, in the ghostly gaze of old photos from another time and country, in the violent eruption of dormant emotions, in the fragmentariness of stories more mythic than real: for those of us born after, the war lives on like a collapsed and nebulous star, emitting its spectral light across generational and historical distance, and transmitting encoded messages across vast expanses of silence.

For Nguyen Huu Hong Minh, "A Historical Black Hole" warps all social reality in postwar Vietnam. In his controversial poem of the same name, the self is seen from the perspective of the collective, including a virtual tour of the major cities, rivers, and regions of the country, but the poem's representation of the national body politic becomes increasingly sexual, violent, solipsistic, and scatological. In this way, the poem wildly perverts the preoccupations of socialist realism. The poet, who "sees his male member in Saigon, / His head in Hanoi / His arms and legs abandoned somewhere in Soc Trang [....] His soul hung from some pubic hair of a Hai Phong girl whoring in China," finds not progress and development, but inertia and degradation; no revolutionaries and acts of heroism, but hedonists and sexual deeds. Evacuating the historical from a long history of violence, Nguyen Huu Hong Minh's poetic provocation from his second-generation perspective is to suggest that there is an important connection to be made between the presence of social disarray in postwar Vietnam and the absence of genuine historical knowledge.

For Nguyen Quoc Chanh, whose poems show a similar negation of and antagonism for postwar Vietnamese society, the poet mourns for the dead who go unmourned and unmemorialized: "I carry a cemetery inside my body." For

Phan Nhien Hao, this means being committed to "memory's bullets." Perhaps no other poet of the postwar generation confronts the difficult, complex legacy of the war as consistently, dramatically and provocatively as Phan Nhien Hao. "Assume this position for a beautiful shot" says a voice suspended between past and present in "A Photo from the 60s." Reflecting upon the fate of a forgotten relative found in an old family photo, Hao constructs through uncertain speaking perspectives and disquieting images a fragmented portrait of lost time and wasted lives:

> In the photo his watch showed 10:05,
> in what must have been a beautiful day
> the young man solemnly sat in front of the camera.
> As the light flashed
> from the darkness of the camera lens the war could just make out
> a young person to lay waste.

Hao's concluding lines give little closure and less consolation. In reopening the wounds of the past, his poems may often achieve a unity of thought and emotion, but are still unreconciled, uncertain, and ambiguous in their shifts in image and metaphor, breaks in line and syntax, and juxtaposition of real and surreal elements. In the name of difficult truths and repressed histories, Hao ultimately refuses, in concert with many other poets in this anthology, the balm and sutures of reconciliation. In poetry of diverse forms of attention, perception and feeling, this postwar generation of poets explore what it means to inherit competing and often contradictory versions of the past and forge a future out of that work of inheritance.

5 /

Paris changes! But nothing of my melancholy has lifted.
—Baudelaire

The most dramatic transformation to affect Vietnam in the last thirty years has arguably been the period of liberalization referred to as *doi moi* or "renovation." In 1986, the Vietnamese Communist Party began implementing a series of open-door economic policies designed to decentralize the economy and transition the country towards a more market-driven model. In the cultural sphere, the state loosened its grip on artists and writers, allowing for a greater degree of creative freedom, and even encouraging social criticism. Thanh Thao's *Rubik's Cube* (1985), Nguyen Quoc Chanh's *Night of the Rising Sun* (1990), and Van Cam Hai's *Man Who Tends The Waves* (1995) all emerged during this period. No longer officially bound to the aesthetic doctrines of socialist realism, more poets and writers felt safe and free to explore forms and themes once set aside as irrelevant or attacked as illegitimate: official corruption, the social consequences of war, the break-down of traditional values, and personal subjectivity, to name a few. Indeed, it must be admitted that poets currently living in Vietnam write about these and other private and public matters with a frequency, intensity, and audaciousness difficult to imagine before or without the cultural impact of the renovation years.

However, it must also be admitted that "privatization in the field of culture and communication," as writer Pham Thi Hoai has skeptically observed, ultimately "has not advanced as far or as radically as the privatization of toilet paper, dish detergent, liquid soap, shampoo, bath soap, toothpaste and tampons." Much of the post-Renovation poetry of *The Deluge* is awash with references to the new goods, products, images, and ideas inundating Vietnam as the country steers through the transformations of globalism. Almost everywhere you go in Vietnam today, bright billboards and colorful street signs celebrate unprecedented growth and development, commemorate national unity and liberation, promote necessary policies to help curb societal problems, and cast Vietnam as the Asian tourist destination of the future. Not celebratory, but critical, many of the poets in this anthology sully the disinfected portrayals of post-Renovation Vietnam. Their poems overflow with disgust, disillusionment, angst, and alienation, tottering dangerously on the edge of violence—in other words, distress signals of a collective unconscious in a moment of cultural crisis.

One of the strongest signals has long been transmitted by Saigon poet Nguyen Quoc Chanh. Despite signs of regeneration during the Renovation years, Chanh's receptive poems detect, as in the following title and lines of one, the "Low Pressure System" affecting Vietnamese society: "I hear cries of a newborn. / A fish crawls out from a bloody hollow. / The woman closes her thighs and a corpse is covered up." With lines like this, Chanh tested the limits of the open door policy towards Vietnamese writers. Ever since his emergence during the Renovation years, Chanh has been fearless in his criticism of the government and unapologetic in his experimentation with poetic form. In effect, he has found himself and his work slandered and shut out of mainstream literary magazines and state-run publishing houses. Like many poets writing in Vietnamese, Chanh now publishes his work almost exclusively in online literary journals. Consequently, his poetry can be read online by someone in Cabramatta in western Sydney, Australia, but not by someone browsing the poetry shelves in a bookstore in Ho Chi Minh City.

Such a stifling atmosphere gives further credence to Pham Thi Hoai's critical assessment of the impact of Renovation on the Vietnamese literary landscape during the mid-1990 until today. According to Hoai,

> The post-Renovation period is indeed one of strange empty spaces, of absent authority, of a train without an engine or an engineer. The old prestige of ideology, of systems of thought and of certain spiritual values, have been abandoned, but the empty spaces have been sealed shut, leaving no opportunity for new sources of prestige or value to take their place.

These are precisely the "strange empty spaces" Nguyen Quoc Chanh's poetry seems to evoke and manifest in its complex system of images, allusions, and syntax. Unlike Hoai, Chanh doesn't see the total absence of authority in post-war, post-Renovation Vietnam. Rather, part of Chanh's poetic project is to reveal the places where power and authority still resides and hides—in our language, in our bodies and minds, in our relations to others and ourselves—as he provocatively suggests in a more recent poem aptly titled, "Post, Post, but not Post...":

> Straight on: my face's blank.
> Aslant: my face's askew.
> Below or above: my face's equally messed up.
>
> Next to a Cambodian: I'm gloriously yellow.
> Next to a Westerner: I flatten myself in panic.
> Next to a Chinese. I timidly squint.

"The poet makes himself a *visionary* through a long, a prodigious and rational disordering of *all* the senses," wrote Rimbaud. All the senses are deployed and disordered in the poetry of Chanh, unacknowledged visionary of new Vietnamese poetry.

6 /

I walk on bridges connecting two alien shores
— Phan Nhien Hao

Part literary geography, *The Deluge* maps a global diaspora of poetry in Vietnamese. Nearly half of the poets in this anthology live in countries other than Vietnam. Thanh Tam Tuyen emigrated to the U.S. in 1983 after his release from seven years of imprisonment, eventually resettling in Minnesota. After his release from twelve years of imprisonment in 1988, Tran Da Tu received political asylum in 1989 from the Swedish government and settled in California with his wife, the poet and novelist Nha Ca. Like countless Vietnamese, Khe Iem escaped Vietnam by boat in 1988, spending a year in a Malaysian refugee camp before coming to California in 1989, where he would eventually edit an influential Vietnamese journal of poetry. Others live in places as remote as De Kalb in rural northern Illinois and in cities as cosmopolitan as London, Tokyo, and Paris.

But can Vietnamese poets living abroad contribute to the creation of a new Vietnamese poetry? This question was posed to Nguyen Duy, a well-known, award-winning poet living in Vietnam. "I cannot imagine a hyphenated poetry—half Vietnamese and half English or some other language. Poetry can't be created via bi-national marriages or artificial insemination," replied Duy, "Vietnamese poets living abroad can act as a bridge between Vietnamese poetry and world poetry. It's a contribution befitting the circumstance of the time. But whether contemporary Vietnamese poetry can create a new departure is something that will be determined by poets living in the homeland." So much for the expansive view of poetry. Duy speaks of poetry as if it were a remote country with a monolithic culture, heavily fortified borders, and limited foreign policy. He doesn't suffer from a failure of imagination so much as a hyperactive one: a fantasy of a purely Vietnamese poetry that relies on the greater fantasy of a purely Vietnamese language. Both serve to perpetuate and protect certain political aims and vested interests connected to nationalism and national literature. To imagine something like "a hyphenated poetry" after all would mean letting go of such territorial and authoritarian claims to a "Vietnamese poetry...determined by poets living in the homeland."

For now, never mind the countless cases of exile and émigré writers of the twentieth century; ignore the number of influential Vietnamese writers currently living abroad (Duong Thu Huong, Pham Thi Hoai, and Tran Vu to name a few); forget the fact that the production and reception of contemporary literature in Vietnamese is no longer located solely in Vietnam, but emanates from places like Westminster and Paris, and with the advent of the Internet, networked through online literary journals like Berlin-based *Talawas* (the name of Pham Thi Hoai's journal a Vietnamese-German mongrelization for "we-are-what") and Sydney-based *Tienve* (whose expressed mission is "to contribute to the formation of a Commonwealth of Vietnamese Arts, where, regardless of geographical and political differences, artistic creativity is reunited with its original meaning, namely, the making of the new")—read the poets in this anthology and you'll witness a new departure for poetry in Vietnamese, created by poets not only living in Vietnam but around the globe.

Consider the case of Phan Nhien Hao. Coming of age in Vietnam after 1975, Hao immigrated to the United States in 1991. While he currently lives and works in the U.S., he continues to write his poetry in Vietnamese. As he writes in the poem "Excavations," "At sunrise, I have gathered":

> The breakages of a child growing up during war,
> a contempt of ostentatious games, the enduring loneliness
> of a wandering exile, a half Western-half Vietnamese knowledge.

The "half Vietnamese and half English" does not represent a liability, but rather a source of new poetic material for Hao. His poems are a confluence of different creative currents: the associative jump-cuts of surrealism, the brooding consciousness of Existentialist philosophy, the emotional textures of jazz and blues, the stripped-down language of an American modernist idiom inherited from William Carlos Williams, and the literary legacy of South Vietnamese poets such as Thanh Tam Tuyen.

A defense of poetry of the Vietnamese diaspora can be found throughout the anthology. In "Night Song of Ceylon," cosmopolitan Do Kh, drawing on the dramatic voice of the lyric, empathetically imagines the life and work of female migrant laborers, "Boarding the airplane at 4:25 AM / To change pillowcases, empty ashtrays and pick up blankets." In "Monolinguist with Light Pole on Bolsa Avenue," Tran Tien Dung, a resident of Ho Chi Minh City, imagines the experience of being uprooted and adrift in geography and history, "fearing the place of refuge the place escaped from," as he visits for the first time his Vietnamese friends living in the U.S. In his two poems "Echo from a Puddle" and "A Crack in the Wall," Ai Van Quoc employs an economy of line and image evocative of classical Chinese and Japanese poetic traditions, creating a cross-cultural archeology of allusions to Japanese, Vietnamese, Chinese, and Western civilizations. Like Ai Van Quoc, who has translated several Japanese and Chinese poets into Vietnamese, including Shuntaro Tanikawa, Bei Dao, and Ye Hui, a number of the poets here are also active translators: Nguyen Dang Thuong has translated poems, plays and short stories from Neruda, Cendrars, Prevert, Beckett, Claude Simon, Rimbaud, Stein, Bukowski and many others; Phan Nhien Hao has translated a number of American poets (Robert Lowell, William Carlos Williams) into Vietnamese, as well as Linh Dinh's fiction; Thanh Thao has co-translated Boris Pasternak. The case of these and other poets give ample evidence to Trinh Thanh Thuy's assertion: "Influenced by the peculiarities of foreign languages and cultures, Vietnamese texts written overseas do not lose their strengths but gain new dimensions through awakened, previously latent capabilities."

7 /

look for a new brand tomorrow
—Lynh Bacardi

But you don't have to go overseas to see how Vietnamese poetry is being shaped by outside influences. Some of the most provocative entries in the day book and dream log of contemporary Vietnam belong to a controversial group of poets based in Ho Chi Minh City known as *Mo Mieng* or "Open Mouth." Represented at the end of this anthology by its three leading exponents, Bui Chat, Ly Doi and Lynh Bacardi, the so-called Open Mouth poets (the English elides the command form—"open your mouth" or "open wide"—implied in the Vietnamese) have attracted considerable attention for writing poetry unfit for print. Despite all the shock value attached to them, the relevance of the Open Mouth poets rests not in what their poems say about them as individuals, per se, but what their poetry illicitly reports, as suggested in this poem of the same title by Bui Chat, on the "Kurrent State" of Vietnamese society—

> nothin kan seize me from da hands
> a look doesn't korrespond to da fi fingers
> between da rite and left eyes
> not da blue runny nose
> dis world kannot squeeze me
> old images alter me same as new

—and in these lines from Lynh Bacardi's "Shrink & Stretch":

> outside all living things are in mourning clothes and trampling on each other to reach heaven. I uncouth a building built with virginal blood. feigning an orgasmic moan. sunlight high above weeping inundating the streets. men who become bloodless when overburdened. the obese rain flows hotly. I'm pregnant with coins reeking a burning smell. a mother selling her flow keeping the cultural flow for her brood...today all ideas upset the stomach.

The grossly sexual, scatological, violent, taboo, mundane, and dream life—all make their way into poems by Bui Chat, Ly Doi, and Lynh Bacardi. In their eyes, nothing is too base because everything has been debased. Rejecting social norms and aesthetic forms of authority, the nihilism of the Open Mouth poets retaliates against the chaotic cohabitation of the Communist regime, Confucian values, and Capitalist materialism in contemporary Vietnam. These three political, social and economic forces are the alternating targets of ridicule in Ly

Doi's prose poems: the two poems from "Seven Spider Improvisations" mock the coercive aura of ancient Confucian teachings; "Society 3" takes aim at the absurd levels of corruption permeating Vietnamese society; and "The Benefits of Poetry" levels a critique of the crass commercialism overtaking Vietnam.

Literary vandalism might be a better way to describe what they're up to—breaking, destroying, and effacing our more precious ideas of poetic form, content, and language. Hence, the Hip-Hop cadenced, Vietnamese street-slang of Bui Chat's vernacular lyrics; the social critique of Ly Doi's collage poems drawing on newspaper, advertisement and internet sources, and the aleatory swerve of perception in Lynh Bacardi's prose poems. Their indecorous poems reveal, and to the extent which such conditions offer grounds for creativity, give ambivalent expression to the decay, depravity, and decadence surrounding them.

A medieval hilltop town in Tuscany is unlikely to appear anywhere on anyone's literary map of contemporary Vietnamese poetry. But it was in Certaldo, Italy where I first met Linh in February of 2004. I was in Europe on a fellowship at the time and discovered that he was living in Certaldo as a guest of the now defunct International Parliament of Writer's Cities of Asylum network. I took the train down from Paris. We decided to meet in the Piazza Boccaccio, named after Certaldo's most famous resident and the author of *The Decameron*. It was raining. I waited for Linh beside the statue of Boccaccio and leaned against his stone cape for shelter. Across from me was an old cathedral, unremarkable except for its immense wooden doors, which seemed immovable to me at first, until I watched them open and slowly release a cortege of mourners. That's when Linh appeared, greeting me and pointing to the funeral just in case I might have missed it. We left the procession to its own workings and proceeded up the steep road to Linh's residence at 2 Via Valdracca, just inside the old city walls. I ended up staying for ten days.

In the course of our nightly conversations, he often circled back to the topic of contemporary Vietnam and Vietnamese poetry. Shortly before his Italian journey, he had lived in Vietnam for two and a half years, between 1999 and 2001. I listened as he spoke of the literary scene in Ho Chi Minh City, his affection and admiration for certain poets there, the official verse culture in Vietnam, his disdain of the suffocating role played by the Writer's Union. Relearning Vietnamese, Linh began translating many of the poets he was reading and meeting on a daily basis. In many ways, the present anthology is an extraordinary record of these real and imagined engagements.

It is sometimes forgotten that the group of seven women and three men who gather in a villa in the Tuscan countryside to tell the one hundred stories that make up Boccaccio's *Decameron* had just fled plague-ridden Florence. The humorous and often bawdy tales they tell stand in stark contrast to Boccaccio's haunting and unflinchingly detailed portrayal of the effects of the Black Plague at the beginning of book. Yet the backdrop of the Plague creates the conditions necessary for their stories. Through the species of refuge called the poem, the poets gathered in this anthology similarly write in flight from catastrophe. Not as escape artists, but in order to create a collective counterforce to oppressive realities.

Hai-Dang Phan
Gainesville, Florida
April 2011

THANH TAM TUYEN was born in Vinh, northern Vietnam, in 1936, moved to Saigon in 1954, emigrated to the US in 1983, and died in Minnesota in 2006. Drafted into the Army of the Republic of Vietnam, he served two stints, 1962-1966, then from 1968 until the end of the war in 1975. He was imprisoned for seven years in remote Yen Bai by the victorious Hanoi government. His first and most famous poetry collection, *Tôi không còn cô độc* [*I'm No Longer Desolate*], was released in Saigon in 1956. That same year, he co-founded, with Mai Thao, the groundbreaking literary journal *Sáng Tạo* [*Creativity*]. Much admired and very influential in South Vietnam, Thanh Tam Tuyen introduced a cleaner, starker music into Vietnamese poetry, and was the first Viet poet to write about jazz. Besides poetry, he also published a play, essays, four novels and three collections of short stories.

Resurrection

I want to cry like I want to vomit
on the street
crystal sunlight
I call my own name to soothe my longing
thanh tam tuyen
evening a star breaks against a church bell
I need a secret place to kneel
for a little boy's soul
fearful of a fierce dog
a hungry dog without colors

I want to die like I want to sleep
although I'm standing on a river bank
the deep dark water is restless
I scream my own name to slake my rage
thanh tam tuyen
night falls onto a sinful whispering realm
O child wearing a red kerchief
Hey there wolf
a wandering sort of wolf

I crave suicide
an eternal sort of murderer
I scream my own name in distress
thanh tam tuyen
strangle myself into collapsing
so I could be resurrected
into an ongoing string of life
mankind doesn't forgive the crime of murder
the executioners kneel
the time of resurrection

a shout is a prayer
for the waiting centuries
I want to live like I want to die
among intersecting breaths
a flaming chest
I call softly
dear
open the door to your heart
my living spirit has turned into a child
as pure as the truth one time.

Thanh Tam Tuyen

Definition of a Good Poem

more than a species of frightful crow
white curtain a worried finger rubbing the eye
let's drop it into the sky's evening
a life as round as a green rice flake
third season of a year dripping milk
as lucky as a poem with agreeable consonants

syllogism needed
a man must die
you're a man so you must die
a public notice
sleep children the hearts of loved ones
a sacred journey without end conducted with blood

how many creative works completed
only to be summed up with a spoken word
you should use your work to say farewell to everyone

a line of poetry as good as a saying
a good poem is the final death

so long the bed the table the chair
one person two persons three persons

one person two persons three persons

In the Name of

Au nom du front parfait profond—Eluard

An imperfect love
Inside the soul of each eye
A shameful life

A mute chest without voice
Lips without laughing substance
Starving senses

An alley night surrounding window
A seated person forgetting time
Emotions demanding an exit

A free barren hand
Flowers declining youthful hair
Measured breaths

The survival of one person
The survival of many people
Innocent people

In the name of
Love freedom man
I have the right to call forth

Those who have died to show up
Those still alive to raise their hands

Thanh Tam Tuyen

Black

A black person a black snatch of singing
A black sky without end
Streams of tears
Shredding the body with sounds of a silver horn
With the voice of blood of marrow of the soul at the beginning
In the jungle without speech endless jungle empty
Throwing self throwing the crowd into nakedness shame resentment of the
body
Yesterday and today shattered much less tomorrow
Yet not to be forgotten could not be forgotten
Because Blues is not blue because Blues is black
On a sobbing skin color
In a night club
Starting to bleed in secret crying in your throat
Fingers pinching a horn as if it was a talisman
Choosing beyond the body beyond love beyond hate
Choosing a world of colliding metals beckoning
Soft time
Not running into time
Space spinning into circles of memory
Then one day Blues would reappear as blue.

Three-Quarter Time

for Doan Quoc Si

A round bullet hole on your chest
A bayonet through the lung
Heart still beating
In three-quarter time
Love, freedom forever
You return to sit in your garden
Trees form fruits immediately
Flowers sprinkling cover your body
You run in double-time over obstacles
Eyes glowing
Unification freedom
In the distant city
Wheels roll in three-quarter time
A blue shirt eagerly
Brings down the hammer
Loosens the spinning machine
Doors try to outgrow each other
In three-quarter time
Love freedom forever
Lapping water adding layers of silt
Rice paddies bloom
Tall mountains bending trees
In three-quarter time
Love freedom forever
The nation land and water
In relentless rhythm
Hanoi Hue Saigon
Sobbing in each other's arms
Holding a gun someone shoots at the head
Bullets exploding in three-quarter time
Not dead
You sit up suddenly
Strangely healthy
Someone's ringing steps
In three-quarter time
Love
Freedom
forever
Love freedom forever
Love freedom
forever O my brother

Sitting

For Ngoc Dung AKA the prince of Chi Hoa

Towards evening strolling to the cemetery.
Low hanging autumn weather no scent but the raw grass.
Inside red-flecked eyes a corner of the summer sky smolders.
Rows of snaggly tombstones behind me on the lush fading lawn.
At the foot of the hill a neighborhood behind thin woods.
Sitting to watch. Sitting to reflect.
A cool breeze blowing chunks of my mind away.
Sitting as if planted by the gods. I plant this meat sack.
Sleeping wide-eyed without knowing it.

30/06/2000

PHUNG CUNG (b. Son Tay 1928; d. Hanoi 1997) was one of the youngest members of the dissident literary movement, Nhan Van Giai Pham, active in North Vietnam from 1955 to 1958. He became famous through the 1956 allegorical short story, "Lord Trinh's Old Horse," which ridiculed prominent writers for mechanically mouthing Party propaganda. In 1962, he was arrested by the Communist government and jailed for twelve years without charge. He re-emerged in 1994 with the poetry collection, *Watching The Night*, which caused a sensation in the Vietnamese literary community worldwide. His poems have been translated into English and published in the journal *The Literary Review*.

Luckily

Luckily while out
Walking this morning
I encountered only
BEAUTIFUL people
Ecstatic
And in tears
I wanted to carpet the lane
With my back.

Clumsy

Hatless
Shoeless
Clumsy in career
Dragging a shadow
Dirty body clean shadow
Night and day facing
Kids

Night Pond

A guest wind arrived
The wild flower a nimble pen
The water surface blue and black
Drew—erased—drew
Something mysterious
Late night at the pond's edge
The firefly searched with its light
For the decorative touch.

Phung Cung

Visiting a Grave

A fistful of bones suspended in earth
Can't even see it
A small breeze—violet thistles
Latching on—memories
Violet—an evening looking northwest.

Wanton

The benevolent ground
A wanton sole not yet tired
A bamboo roof poking into the drifting
purple sunset

A letter to an old friend
Mistakenly sent to a frigid alley
The wind busily shifts to a new season
Cuddling all the months and years.

NGUYEN DANG THUONG was born in Battambang, Cambodia in 1938, and now lives in London, England. He has translated poems, plays and short stories from Neruda, Cendras, Prevert, Beckett, Claude Simon, Rimbaud, Stein, Bukowski and many others into Vietnamese. His poems and translations appear regularly on <tienve.org>. English translations of his work have been published in *Of Vietnam: Identities in Dialogue* (Palgrave 2001) and the webzine *Fascicle*. Nguyen Dang Thuong comments: "I don't write poetry out of sadness. I become sad from writing poetry. To me, a finished poem is a corpse, a published poem a mummy." Playful, provocative and at times silly, he's the ageless enfant terrible of Vietnamese poetry.

Orthotics For Easter

With a body sewn up just last night
assembled with a pig's heart a cow's lungs nylon hair
fake teeth & hands from a corpse of a
white *serial killer* & facial skin
grafted from a buttock & limbs of pink plastic
bones & flesh & an all-seeing eye
my brain is a computer chip I design
programs of lasting happiness for the future
I look back at my life O it is so new
so gorgeous so perfect I'm grateful
O danke schön herr doktor frankenstön

Nguyen Dang Thuong

The Artist

He swallowed ten white mice in five minutes the audience didn't applaud.
He disrobed and twisted himself into yoga positions sucked his own dick the
audience didn't cheer. He pulled out a sword to disembowel himself exposing
his guts and liver the audience wasn't terrified. In the end, he gave up. O, only
that and it's already dusk? I still don't have a lover and am living in the most
magnificent and desolate city on earth.

Magic Realism—Or: Greetings

In 1974 something bizarre happened to me after I had just arrived in Paris. My very first evening I wandered down to St-Germain-des-Pres to look for the bar where Sartre and Simone hung out. I had just gotten off the Metro and was looking lost on the street when I saw a large Frenchman as handsome as Christopher Reeves in Superman. The large Frenchman wearing a large suit glanced at me with emotion then headed straight for a small public restroom nearby. Curious I followed him. O astonishment of astonishment! Before me was a giant statue by Michelangelo as silky white as a fairy. But between his buttocks as pale pink as breasts on a male figure as cute as a dream a pig tail appeared to stick out though I wasn't quite sure. Finally I gathered enough courage to ask superman: Greetings in the middle of Paris. What's that knob up front and what's that in the back?

Nguyen Dang Thuong

43

TRINH CONG SON was a famous song writer whose lyrics were certainly poetry. He was born in Daklak in 1939, grew up in Huế, studied in Qui Nhơn, taught school in Bảo Lộc, then finally moved to Saigon in 1965, where he became famous. He wrote over 600 songs, achieving his first hit, "Ướt mi" ["Wet Lashes"], in 1957. Joan Baez dubbed him Vietnam's Bob Dylan. In Tran Anh Hung's film "Vertical Ray of the Sun," he shares the soundtrack with Lou Reed, Arab Strap and The Married Monk. Pretty good company, yes, and a nice comparison, but Trinh Cong Son was always his own man. To the South Vietnamese government, he was way too left, but to the Communists, he wasn't red enough. He survived the Vietnam War, only to be condemned to hard labor for four years. When he died in 2001, from diabetes, liver and kidney failure, from decades of boozing, it seemed that all of Saigon showed up for his funeral. Tragic, resigned and romantic, his songs embody the atmosphere of wartime Saigon, especially when they're sung by the soulful, husky-voiced Khanh Ly, with her bluesy, heart-wrenching phrasings.

Sand and Dust

Which grain of dust became my flesh
To blossom and rise up someday
O marvelous sand and dust
The sun lights a wandering fate

Which grain of dust became my flesh
So I could become dust someday
O exhausted sand and dust
What beating noise that won't cease

How many years playing a human role
Then one evening, hair white as lime
Yellow leaves falling from on high
A hundred years dying in a day

Which sun illuminates my heart
So love could be mashed to pebbles
Please let me hide my face in sorrow
As I wait for happy news each day

(1965)

Like Bittern Wings Flying

Is sunlight as pink as your lips?
The rain as sad as your eyes?
Your hair in each small fiber
Fallen into life makes waves drift

The wind will exult at your hair flying
Let pouting clouds doze on your shoulders
Your skinny small shoulders
Like bittern wings flying far off

Is the sunlight still jealous of your lips?
The rain still sad in those clear eyes?
From the moment I took you home
I knew we'd be separated for good

The spring greets your footsteps passing
Leaves sing from the fragrant hands
Leaves will wither from waiting
Like a human life forever overcast

Is it cheerful where you're going?
Is the sky blue where you're going?
I hear a thousand teardrops
Falling, creating a sparkling lake

(1964)

TRAN DA TU was born in 1940 in Hai Duong, northern Vietnam, went to Saigon in 1954 during the partition of the country, where he later became a journalist and prominent poet. During 1963, he was imprisoned by the Ngo Dinh Diem government for his dissident views. After 1975, he was imprisoned for 12 years by the Communists. His wife, the famous novelist and poet Nha Ca, the only South Vietnamese female writer among 10 black-listed as "cultural guerrillas" by the Communist regime, was also imprisoned from 1976-1977. In 1989, a year after Tran Da Tu was released from prison, the couple and their children received political asylum from the Swedish government, but later moved to the US and now live in Southern California. Tran Da Tu has published two volumes of poems in Vietnam before 1975, *When I Wrote Love Poems for You* (*Thuở làm thơ yêu em*, 1960) and *Declaring Love in the Night* (*Tỏ tình trong đêm*, 1965). A third volume, *A Hundred Year Smile* (*Nụ cười trăm năm*, 1990), written in the U.S., remains unpublished. The critic Thuy Dinh writes, "Like most South Vietnamese writers of the same generation, i.e., Doan Quoc Sy, Duong Nghiem Mau, Nguyen Manh Con, Tran Da Tu considered himself "old before his time" because of the time he lived in. His generation's literary outputs were seen as too solipsistic, too philosophical, too "existentially ambivalent," in Nguyen Ba Chung's description. From the Communist perspective, Tran Da Tu and his urbane, subversive, chain-smoking circle of friends were viewed as too full of themselves and too negative to divert or prevent the U.S. imperialist policy in the South." Although somewhat neglected for a time, it's becoming clearer than ever that Tran Da Tu's one of the leading Vietnamese poets of his generation.

Love Tokens

I'll give you a roll of barbwire
A vine for this modern epoch
Climbing all over our souls
That's our love, take it, don't ask

I'll give you a car bomb
A car bomb exploding on a crowded street
On a crowded street exploding flesh and bones
That's our festival, don't you understand

I'll give you a savage war
In the land of so many mothers
Where our people eat bullets and bombs instead of rice
Where there aren't enough banana leaves to string together
To replace mourning cloths for the heads of children

I'll give you twenty endless years
Twenty years seven thousand nights of artillery
Seven thousand nights of artillery lulling you to sleep
Are you sleeping yet or are you still awake

On a hammock swinging between two smashed poles*
White hair and whisker covering up fifteen years**
A river stinking of blood drowning the full moon
Where no sun could ever hope to rise

I'm still here, sweetie, so many love tokens
Metal handcuffs to wear, sacks of sand for pillows
Punji sticks to scratch your back, fire hoses to wash your face
How do we know which gift to send each other
And for how long until we get sated

Lastly, I'll give you a tear gas grenade
A tear gland for this modern epoch
A type of tear neither sad nor happy
Drenching my face as I wait.

Saigon, 1964

Translator's notes:
*An allusion to the shape of Vietnam
**The age when he started publishing poetry

Tran Da Tu

Toy for Future Children

A blind and deaf bullet buried in the field
Dozing through decades of blood and bones
Then one morning
In a bustling future
As the children return to the field
Returning to goof around and chase each other

The blind and deaf bullet will be dug up
Will be dug up and awaken
In the middle of this happiness
As the children shriek and crow
The bullet will wake up
Wake up and open its eyes
Open its eyes and explode
Explode and the children will die
Die with their bodies and faces shattered

There, that's the toy left over by your parents

O my children
What more can I say
What can say to my children, to my children
To a pitiful future.

Saigon, 1964

50

Fragmented War

The loose change are still warring on the table
Amid paint brushes, useless plays, poems and bits of paper

The long war, the miserable scraps of food
A weird adventure inside a bowl's rim
How do we exit from it
Beside stripping ourselves naked
To search and sketch ourselves, to confess
Is there a body not as obscure as the night
A desire not as messy as a storm

That's when history assumes the enemy's face
I punch his chin hurting my hand
Hear love dissolving like a breath exhaling
While the past is as exhausted as an illusion
As you look down
How do we exit from it
Beside finding each other
To weep, lament and swap stories
Is there a history not as treacherous as you
A truth not as ragged as mother
These are mornings you must stand on the balcony
Evenings you must wander the streets
Suns that must be put into frames
Nights that must appear as words
And how can we exit from it
Beside dying
So as to finish, fall and exterminate ourselves.

Saigon, 1965

So Long Tuong

So long Tuong, so long Tuong
Morning in an orb
Evening in a tube
A liquid life

So long Tuong, so long Tuong
Handfuls of earth covering up
So long Tuong, so long Tuong
A treacherous wheel
The sun red then yellow
Cursed days

So long Tuong, so long Tuong
Summer in the sky
Summer out at sea
Summer in the city, in the blood
So long Tuong, so long Tuong
Handfuls of earth covering up

So long Tuong, so long Tuong
Ca Na, Phan Thiet,
Chi Lang, the New Bridge neighborhood
Raise your hands close your eyes

So long Tuong so long Tuong
So long Tuong
Handfuls of earth covering up.

Saigon, 1965

Standing

Standing there. Standing on Freedom Street*
Standing beneath the brightest streetlamp
Standing to solicit and to shift back and forth
Standing to gesture and to jiggle
Standing to pant with rubber-stuffed bosom
Standing shamelessly with diseased asset

Standing there. Standing there since when
Since when and until when
O my sisters, how would I know.

Saigon, 1965

Translator's note:
*i.e., Tu Do Street, much frequented by prostitutes servicing American GIs
during wartime

Writing Poetry Tirelessly

Good news, dear, I've recovered
Don't lament, don't comfort me
Share this happiness with me
The way I was happy being ill
Happy to be healthy

I must share this happiness with you
Don't you know
The way I made you share with me
So much suffering and injustice
I'm happy now I'm content now
With each meal
I heartily eat three full bowls of rice
Each morning, I heartily take a shower
Do I eat too much
Take a shower too much
Don't chide me, my love
Remember the good news I'm bringing
I've just recovered from illness

You can't be happy with me yet, my love
Why are you so stupid
I'll tell you so many strange tales
How I met the angel of death in my happy bout of illness
The angel of death, dear, sat at the foot of the bed
The angel of death, dear, stood on the mosquito netting
The angel of death, dear, was no less beautiful than you
No less innocent than me
I was so happy, I don't have words to describe it
Look deeply into my eyes
The angel of death in my eyes in my loose clothing
Was filled with a soothing humanity

Do you still remember, my love
The many debts I incurred from you
And those we incurred from others
Where we borrowed one to pay back ten times
Borrowed a hand to pay back so many bodies
Borrowed a streak of tear to pay back oceans
Borrowed a happy smile
To incur so much grief

Of course, my love, how could we forget
The many creditors we had to deal with
Who forced us to grimace in borrowing
To grimace when we were delinquent
To grimace when we repaid

Don't yell at me, my love, for getting off topic
Don't be impatient
I know I'm telling you about the angel of death
I know that I have to be clear so you'd know
The angel of death is really a creditor

Don't be shocked, don't grimace
The angel of death lent us our first baby steps
Then so many years
So many cheerful, colorful candles on birthday cakes
The way I borrowed from the angel of death
So many struggling days and nights and your love

Do you remember, my love
The times we were delinquent with each other
The times we were delinquent with others
Try to remember, I'll tell you
How I was delinquent with the angel of death
I was cheerfully delinquent not sheepish or grimacing
Recognizing me, the angel of death was cordial:
-Ah, you're done already, paying your debt so soon?
-Nah, I'm not done yet, brother
He cordially asked, I cordially answered

And I spoke in a low voice to the angel of death
How you were waiting for my affection to resume
How friends were waiting for my boozing and carousing to resume
How our country and humanity were waiting for my service to resume
And I wanted to chit chat with him even longer
But do you know what happened
The angel of death smilingly opened the register
Smilingly extended my debt
Without fussing over the interest

Do you see, my love
How I still love you, love humanity
Still want to carouse and to serve
The way the angel of death, a humane creditor

Tran Da Tu   55

Still loves us
Still lends us bright candles
To bloom radiantly on your birthday cake
On our small child's birthday cake
On our friends' and humanity's birthday cakes

Do you feel my happiness yet, my love
Let's be sweet like this cake
This fragrant nicely round cake
Waiting for us to share with each other
Let's hop about like a flame
The warm flame of life still burning
Whether it's this place or that place
Still burning, whether this or that person
Still burning, even if the pair of us
Are no more

You received my good news yet, my love
Bring your kiss by the flame
So I can see it clearly
Bring your breath by the cake
So I can swallow with pleasure
Be happy with me, just recovered from illness
The way I'm happy loving you, loving humanity
Happy loving life, loving death

And happy writing poems tirelessly.

[California, after 2000]

TRAN VANG SAO, real name Nguyen Dinh, was born in Hue in 1942, where he now lives. His father was killed by the French during the First Indochina War. During the Vietnam War, Vang Sao was a contributor to the underground newspaper "Youths Against America." He joined the National Liberation Front in 1965, lived in areas under its control, broadcasting propaganda until 1969, when he was injured and removed to the north. In spite of his allegiance to the Communist cause during the war--his pen name, "Vang Sao," means "Yellow Star," a reference to the national flag--he has been blacklisted since 1972 for his candid depictions of social conditions inside Vietnam. He's been harassed constantly, even imprisoned, his manuscripts confiscated. Vang Sao's voice is bemused, ironic, deliberately banal, a reaction against the dogmatic bombast of many of his contemporaries. His poems have been translated into English and published in the journals *American Poetry Review* and *The Literary Review*.

I Get To Eat Meat

I let myself imagine a day when I get to eat meat
I laugh and talk cheerfully
a piece of meat with a hunk of fat
                              slips down my throat
my two eyes are wide open
I squat on the floor and
                    a plate with lots of meat in front of my face
long stalks of green onion floating
                              in grease
hand holding chopsticks mouth chewing
the sun blazing through the leaves
an afternoon in summer with no wind

I wake up and scratch my neck
the river water is salty
I go to the end of the alley to smoke a cigarette
then say out loud to myself
it will thunderstorm this evening bringing cool weather

August 19, 1982

Tran Vang Sao

Night

night of screams flowing through the brain stabbed suddenly
                                        in the throat
rain streams down
then silence
no winds
no sounds of dripping water
emptied out thwarted

night sneaking behind back in front of face left right over
                                        head below feet
eyes
hats worn snugly
outside windows
in corners of rooms
behind a rotting bamboo partition
shhh!

night oozing blood from fingertips
clawing through garbage
a plastic bag
a torn rag
lumps of rice
pieces of bone
broken bottles rusty cans copper wire

nights of rats and men burrowing inside sewers
under a bridge
in the middle of a market
on a sidewalk
mud
water
sweat
dirt
trash
and
shit

night of flares in the sky men holding flags
                                        running over blood
teeth grinding
faces green with fright

assault slogans
arms thrusting skyward
K57 DKB F105 B40 AR15 AK M113 T54
people dying
people living
people laughing
people crying

1975

night of demonstrations on the streets
tanks hand grenades concertina barb wires
masks and hunting dogs

night during war staying up to watch a corpse

night of B52 vomiting chemicals

night in 1968
night of espionage
night of conspiracies
night of assassinations
night of suicides
night of kidnappings
night of executions
night of hurrahs
night of denouncements
night of prison
night of blood
night of hunger
night of escaping overseas
night gouges the eyes of a mute man
night of Satan chewing the Eucharist
        face turned skyward laughing absolving sins

night of a number eight storm
night of hands clasped together in prayer
night of escaping overseas

night and morning after misty rain over a pile of human shit
night of getting up in the middle of sleep to watch night
night with last night's ghosts hovering before door
night of mice squeaking in someone else's house
night of cats fighting on roof

night of male grasshopper having head bitten off
night of whores chasing bad luck
     in front of the Teacher's College
burning raw salt glue and a stub broom
obscure night of adultery
night of you fragrant and intoxicating
night of one who has lost his mind wearing a mask of a saint
     hiding in the dark to scare children just for fun
night calm without winds
night and me alone in night
night not yet over
already the sounds of children banging on drums
             the unicorn dance

October 17, 1990

The Bottle-Blower

the bottle-blower blows a bottle through a hole
the bottle-blower blows nothing into something
the bottle-blower blows nothing to hold something
the bottle-blower cannot blow the bottle's substance
                              only its shape
the bottle-blower blows himself into the bottle

Taking The Wife To Give Birth

a morning in May I took you to give birth
it was during rice harvesting season it had drizzled
I'm happy you had an easy birth
and a boy
the trees on both sides of the road were still wet
mother lit a bunch of incense sticks to thank
         the sky the earth and our ancestors

my wife lay breathing on the birth table
her belly big and round
I'm a man with nothing to do I stood outside
smoking a cigarette and peering in
I can't remember anything
two upturned metal dippers by a water tank
a few pebbles beneath the eaves
it won't rain anymore
I squatted I stood up I smoked a cigarette I looked back and
forth
my wife lay breathing on the birth table
her belly big and round
a window opened brightly before her face
the banana leaves in a nearby garden showed drops of water
I heard the voices of two women from inside the room
a truck's engine crackling on Thuan An Street
and the sound of a child crying
I stepped onto the threshold
the two women looked at me and smiled
I walked home
there was a light breeze among the leaves
I said out loud to myself
it won't be sunny for a while yet

Hearsays

this one croaked
named Nguyen Van He
eight years old
cassava poisoning
dead three days before his mother knew
      rites performed by neighbors

Tran Van Ha
forty years old
four children
hoeing in the mountain
hand grenade blew up
died
wife and children could not get there in time for funeral

person lying here
a man without known
name age home village
died wearing a Puppet-Army shirt
a pair of brown woman's pants
lain face down five meters from railroad tracks
face beaten flat no eyes nose hands or feet

dead person here
twenty six years old
shot
a bullet through the head
first and last name: Pham Van Te
reason: committed a robbery then ran
did not stop when called

Nguyen Han
thirty nine years old
stabbed self in throat
      with a broken bottle of orange soda
some said because of madness
did say before death
nowadays
there's not even shit to eat

Tran Vang Sao

Nguyen Thi Shorty
thirty four years old
Le Van E thirteen years old
Le Thi Muon ten years old
Le Van Thuoc six years old
Le Thi Ly two years old
suicide by pills
in kitchen
nearby a few warm worm-eaten sweet potatoes
        were found inside a rimless woven basket
note left behind said
too much hardship can't stand it
me and my kids must die

Tran Thi Lan
two and a half years old
sick with no medicine
died

Nguyen Van Lon
forty five years old
starved for too long then ate too much
died
no close relatives

Nguyen Van Thu
twenty six years old
died shirtless on a pile of garbage
in the middle of the market

Nguyen Huu Thuc
fifty years old
died at a banquet table
could not be rushed to hospital
more than a thousand people at funeral

Phan Ngoc The
died during cholera epidemic of 19..
lived to be forty two years old

buried here are four children
approximately six to nine years old
dengue fever
lain dead in market

Pham Huynh Thuong
died at fifty six years old
popped blood vessel
while reading a speech
near the end

November 1982

NGUYEN THI HOANG BAC was born in 1942 in Saigon, and has lived in Virginia since 1985. She is the author of four books of short stories, "Dust Glittering" (1988), "Eroded Side, Packed Side" (1997), "Pull Up the Anchor and Go" (1997) and "Spider."

She published her first story in 1984 while living in a Hong Kong refugee camp with her children. Her poems have appeared in numerous overseas journals, but never gathered into a volume. Her poem, "A Blade of Grass," included here, alludes to a misogynist saying, "A woman pisses lower than a blade of grass." Interviewed by Nguyen Duck Tung, she said, "The fate of Vietnamese women, whether upper or lower class, intellectual or peddling wares on the street, even kept girls, whores and café hostesses… has always moved me. We had to be born and grow up in an Eastern culture that considers it normal to step on women. A woman who could go to school, who try to be educated, who are brilliant at school, exceptional, and who also has an autonomous and independent lifestyle, such a woman is automatically seen as… man-like. The observation itself clearly betrays a prejudice. If a man is perceived as… like a woman, then that would be an insult, no?"

Inspired

this morning the clock   suddenly stood still
I
sometimes
inspired
also want
                        to remove all batteries from life
expansive
I stand
exposed
                        like a clock

1996

A Blade of Grass

urine sound
dripping
inside the bowl splashing
a warm shimmering liquid
                              amber
pouring from my body
that's right
I'm a woman
the type who urinates lower than a blade of grass
now
able to sit haughtily on a bowl
in the future I just might
get bigger and fatter
splashing like rain over
grass nudged by wind

1997

NGUYEN DAT was born in 1945 in Vinh Yen, northern Vietnam, went South in 1954, served in an elite unit of the South Vietnamese Army during the war, and now lives in Ho Chi Minh City. He has published a book of poems, two collections of short stories. His works tend to be gentle, romantically-tinted, never horrific and only occasionally quirky, as in the two poems included here. He has spent a lot of time in Da Lat, a hill station established by the French. With its lakes, rolling hills, pine trees and cool climate, it's the most European town in all of Vietnam. Dat's poems have been translated into English and published in the journal *The Literary Review*.

Early Morning Drama

A Chinese eatery
A reticent Chinese man
A plate of steaming white dumplings.

She looks at me.
When looking at me you should know:
His smile is intended to
His speaking manner represents
His clothing is evidence of
His shoes and sox lead us to believe
She smiles discreetly expressing:
Smiles speaking manners shoes and sox
Teeth Sounds Meat and Bones Bottoms of Feet.

Impotently I get up
Tepid body enervated
Admit He's not attractive
The plate of steaming white dumplings.

Suburban Memories

Summer street
A floor tile incarcerating the footstep
Can it be
Let's just go
Go until exhausted
To go into the field one last option.

Stand still
The forlorn sound of a cricket
The flat rice grain, and
The left-over rice grain
Fall after the bush fire
The trembling of the earth.

Memories etch
The stalled step, and
The mute moment
Death turned out during a night of yearning
Except for him the consolation.

THANH THAO was born in 1946 in Quang Ngai and now lives in Hanoi, where he works as a journalist. He is the author of at least fifteen poetry collections, most notably *The Rubik's Cube* (1985). In 2004, he participated in the 35th Poetry International Festival of Rotterdam, where his poems were translated into Dutch. English translations have appeared in *Drunken Boat* and *Octopus*. Thanh Thao matured under socialist realism and made his name with "A Soldier Speaks of his Generation," a poem in free verse about stoic soldiers enduring the travails of war. By the time Doi Moi came around, he was middle age. Influenced by the Russian Alexander Blok, Pasternak and Essenin, and the Spanish Lorca, Thanh Thao has adopted some modernist tendencies and a patina of surrealism without foraying into the darkest and messiest parts of the subconscious. This sort of measured avant-gardism is not just tolerated by the regime, but encouraged. In an interview, Thanh Thao defends his position: "Frankly, an innovative poet doesn't have to be relentlessly bizarre. Composing poetry, you have to be extremely simple, write as if you're not. There are times to be complex, but you shouldn't always be […] there's no boundary between innovation and tradition. Unlimited innovation will not bring success. There have been trailblazers who sacrificed themselves, but literature, already ruthless, will only take stock of what remains."

In Haste

in haste
facing forgetfulness
facing a sigh
facing movements
facing hopelessness

in haste
without a word of apology
the man steps beyond the branch tip
leaving behind the woman a thin layer of smoke

in haste
the ships seek a harbor
the stars seek a place to be seen
jammed in a puddle
a sudden arch of sky

in haste
lines of poetry seek the flame

Thanh Thao

Serenade

a sun splash at day's end
in winter. Children chasing red clouds
on layers of sky

hope from somewhere you hear me clearly
you of the belated happiness
a small wind flings the door open

no need to understand but feel
through the skin
you of the belated happiness

merging sounds often reverberate
in the night
the variants of your face

merging sounds often return trembling
blurring the face of night

The Sphinx

Who? saying what? the teeth of the wind
in autumn glittering in menace
in the evening back bent against idle thoughts
without ways without questions
the sphinx dives into dinner
in the middle of a dull answer a dull silence
the sphinx peels mysterious layers from its face
like people their clothes
in a fashion show

Anxious Feet

suddenly the tree has anxious feet
see clouds as leaves
winds as branches
roads crisscrossing why do I grow roots
into worries and bustles
into the past
night like a bell sparking round sounds
regretting
night is only the remainder of day
the part for sleep

the world dazzling and strange
chases darkness into a corner
a kind of light appalling and arduous
without pause

clouds are only rags
to patch the sky
stars suddenly become luxuries
people will eventually breed chunks of darkness
each corner of starry night
to sell

The Road Will Lengthen

the road will lengthen become more serene
when he reaches out to touch the white cloud
but when he wants to scream then silence
will have filled up his throat

sowing arid lines of poetry
laboriously planting an entire forest of pines
El Nino

slowly a few inches each year
insensate those who are privileged
with neither treetop nor roots
without happiness growing by the day

I am the tree you have marked
each year a steel collar
circular waves spreading inside the wood
when will the tree recover

the first age ring the first breath
the first kiss a bracing wind
a brief first shudder greenish
at night a dreaming tree wandering

Thanh Thao

A Leaf

I
one of these days
the green tree hands him a leaf
inscribed with a few dim words
as if they share the same last name
down cast at night dusty by day
the leaf has something to say
one of these days

II
a mild sun as if autumn has come
he waits forever
the rose bush sheds its leaves
he waits forever
budding the young shoots
trying to overcome degeneration
starting to revive

Adornments

I will slip a rice stalk on your wrist
a jade bracelet sounds of crickets a leave of grass
a flame of skin and flesh
drowned in a pair of pinkish nipples

I will drape around your neck
the mysterious necklace of night
the clear bells of autumn
tremble as the city flies back towards the sky

I will drape on your chest
a tempest

Possible

plunging into his life
a meteor
igniting on his head
a black flame
the waves pulverize the beach
in the end the sea gulls dip their wings

plunging into his life
a sense of terror
mumbling appeals to the gods
dissolving season withering hour the bell spreads
you cover me
a black flame

A Fire

your soul a slow-blooming flower
I gasp in happiness
returning alone at night
to meet the fire alone

how many years
were the petals shut tight
in boredom
oblivion
bitter misery

I am grateful to the convent
where the fire congealed into a candle
where I wore myself out praying
the body slowly dissolving in the deep night

how many years
the flower-convent-your soul
suddenly burst into flame

Mi Mi

1
my daughter I see you run behind the moon
barking
you are the best dog
barking out shades
footsteps of the clouds
to soothe me on scorching days

2
in life whenever a voice startles
I lean once more on your eyes
brown like the earth

3
lined up in rows the winds
bobbing at dawn
you fly on four feet
the kindest face on a sad day
with ears slightly shuddering the night

4
you absent from the stairs
absent from the air
the house has suddenly become vast
vague the tapping footsteps
you have gone past the wall

5
burying its muzzle into my chest
the night burst into tears

Slow Passage 2000

I

I surround myself
like a dog marking its territory with urine
it's when I surpass limits
the tree tops call. The stars summon
the microbes whisper
a pale ribbon of light pierces the barrier
the woman pushing the trash cart taps onto the evening's face
certain signals
I tidy myself up frantically
in time for the trash cart
sweep everything away
spotless
that's when
the words start to appear like stars

II

a gust of wind tosses
a glare
I contract like a shy plant
fold my leaves
see with thorns
thorns are the plant's tears

a new moon white marble
an empty lot milky moon
dog festival
dogs bark at the moon dogs smile
                            dogs sniff the scent of misfortune
competing at howling their true feelings
those who seek in the night
a task a hope a place of refuge a
                            void
the night promises everything

III

with two pens
two chopsticks
I go search for the spring

slow and tranquil
look the pen is trembling slightly
breathes each stroke of ink
I know that I'm drying up
slow and tranquil

                        IV
youthful days
I spent my days like the rain falling on sand
now I save every leaf
on the branch
the matchbox for the black cricket I use to trap winter's warmth
a bit of summer breeze
the worn match box with a fading label

in front of me a child on crutches learn to walk at 5 in the morning
a truck discharges smoke into the new millennium
a woman who has lost her mind remembers to run towards the street light
                                                behind the dawn's back
the mayflies interrupt their search

                        V
now I know
that other worlds
are also like this

like a bird learning to love its cage
without needing to learn how to sing

                18.3.1999

Hoisting Crane

digging a channel
frog jaw
gouging a hole
holding on
tree roots
tracking worms
swallowing dirt
scooping each pail
dense
slimy
a thousand hearts a thousand lamps
a thousand compressors
limits
dyke breaking
water spilling past doors
I release into you
mesmerized
panting breaths
I go against the seasons rotate the body's clock
hot spot
you mumbling
incantations
scooping each pail
darkness

To Sergei Esenine

Like a rock thrown into the open sea
your poetry provokes deep ripples
Esenine half the autumn of a sunken Russia
following the ship the sailor wanders

and the passengers on that ship
a white tree a puppy a sliver of moon
young girls vodka snow flakes
sank forever with you

beneath linguistic cloudbursts
rolling waves rise dumbly ferociously
the poet lies dreaming at the very bottom
airtight the hull ablaze the sunset

let all those who crave gold and antiques
waste their time diving to salvage
leaves they confuse for gold foils
overlooking grief that sparkles like platinum

is the person lying there a poet or a thief?*
how I love you Esenine
no easy thing to toss away one's life for poetry
or to tie the noose around one's neck

but how can I become healthy
half my life I fly a kite across the sky
the other half is the silent black earth
connected by a flimsy human-thread

but how can I become healthy
cool wind clear moon drunken song and dance
gentle night whose hand is lightly
God is you a vague pair of breasts

1986

* a line of Sergei Esenine "If not a poet
                                   I'd be a thief"

KHE IEM was born in 1946 in Nam Dinh. He escaped Vietnam by boat in 1988, spent a year in a Malaysian refugee camp before coming to California in 1989, where he worked as a delivery man for Domino Pizza. He is the author of the play, "Blood Seed" (1972), the poetry collections, "Youth" (1992) and "Evidence of Home" (1996), and the story collection, "Voice of the Past" (1996). His poems have been translated into English and published in the journals *The Literary Review* and *xconnect*. In 1994, Khe Iem found the influential journal, *Tho*, a tri-quarterly devoted exclusively to poetry. From issue 19 onwards, he started to feature New Formalism in *Tho*. New Formalism was the way of the future, he declared. Free verse was obsolete. In 2004, he even gave up the editorship of *Tho* to devote himself exclusively to promoting New Formalism on his own website. The poems featured here predate his preoccupation with New Formalism.

Choke

to eat   is to choke on si-news   amid   in-
solence   and to inhale   the nu-trient of eye
water   salty   bland lips kissing
sucking   strange gurgling sounds beyond that
madness

Doubt

tears
sun rise
(sun-risen tears)

atmospheric song
wind corrupting
bitter memories

haggling with century about wretchedness
inverted voice, crying buds
tender O familiar heart out in plain
amid thatched roof rain and fire, moon kiss

past washed
to hear hair mist whispering beyond lip is river
flowing abandoned

sitting wild beast
hung dried ragged
nibbling on verdict issuing from source

Inside Realm

irritated
then subdued

indifferent as if never been shipwrecked

eyes emptied
ossified

infuriated by not seeing sunrise
inside realm

Question

bare feet
how strange

always smoking
blowing into evening

to be a minstrel until when
dead standing up

too much

if only not pondering a kiss
in darkness
before birth

while still beyond the sky

Creased

circles spinning over head
circles rolling around feet

to counter inadvertent
silence with a punch
      strolling on
        streets (pissed)
like the wrath of God
              vast

ass thighs and chests. Wild wandering
tight. To drain throat. East and
west. Faces grimacing

creased

Khe Iem

Classified

SPEECH-employ mute technique. Groping
with eyes. Phone. Ask which way to
righteousness.

SELL

Brass. Entrance to food store. Stage
on left. Flirtation or arguments (heroin)
on curb. Open and close in half light. Need
oil lamp.

SORCERY. House rule. Reasonable rates.
Rheumatism and chronic illnesses cured
by light at the end of tunnel. Young moon. Half
concealed, half revealed.

One Second Play

dawn
(again dawn)
mere mention causes jitters

unlit
cigarette

tongue clicked
already trapped

eaves
forlorn

audience where
out there
curtain

Rusty

no radiance
as door opened

combing for an old coin
very old

put coat on
a real gesture

yelling
in a rusty language

Message

wind blinding
inflamed eyes

try my luck

gnaw on
a piece of bread

stand at top of street looking towards

to speak
nothing to say
forget it

remember to go to train station tomorrow
back to where we can bury each other
O.K.

Shrunken Stretched

white world
blank

tasteless

swollen
shrunken stretched

pantomime
over and over

NGU YEN, real name Nguyen Hien Tien, was born in 1952 in Binh Dinh, came to the United States on July 4th, 1975, and now lives in Houston, Texas. He is the author of four books of poems. His pen name means naïve/stupid (ngu) and peaceful/tranquil (yên). He also writes songs, putting to music poems by other poets (always female), and is the founder of Viet Arts, an organization which stages evenings of Vietnamese music and poetry in Houston.

dog dish = my 43rd birthday

I
after 43 years of being a man
like dogs

      This night
      want to be a lowly stray dog howl at the moon
      happily eat left-over
      surprise
      notice that it's very cold up high
      surprise
      bark music
      surprise
      understand that freedom multiplies fate
      surprise
      see beauty feel beauty inherit beauty
      surprise
      forget to love my wife and children
      because I'm a dog

Mother do you know
I had wanted to cry from the time I was five or six
but didn't want the world to think I was in grief
and to ask why are you crying?
do you know mother?:
      tears not because of self-pity
      nor misfortune
      but crying to escape from the mundane
often thought
if you were a dog mother
how smooth my life would be

Please father
sire a dog
with an owner who knows
      how to geld
      a dog doesn't need sex
      psychology
      philosophy

Ngu Yen

howl at the moon
eat trash
then one day
an overcast cold night
insects clinging
germs rising
FINISH

Dear father
please take this bitter cup
and dump it
I only want a dog dish

Do Kh. was born in Haiphong in 1955, went south immediately after, then France in 1968, returned to Saigon in 1973 to join the Army of the Republic of Vietnam, quit after six months, emigrated to France in 1975, later the US, and now divides his time between Paris and California. He was on the editorial board of *Hop Luu* and is the editor of *Thơ*. He is the author of four books: *Rain Making Stick*, short stories (California: Tân Thư, 1989), *Poetry of Do Kh.*, poetry (Tân Thư, 1989), *Things That Piss You Off So Much You Can't Even Talk About Them*, poetry (Tân Thư, 1990) and *Journey to the West*, a travel book (1991). Globe-trotting, with a Lebanese wife, he is the only Vietnamese to write about the Arab World with feelings and authority. His short story, "The Pre-War Atmosphere," is not about the Vietnamese conflict but the Lebanese one. Translated into English, it's included in the anthology *Night, Again: contemporary fiction from Vietnam*. The French translation of another story appeared in *Serpent a Plumes*, the English version in the Prague-based journal *TRAFIKA*. He is also a provocative filmmaker.

Night Song Of Ceylon

We are laborers from Ceylon
Boarding the airplane at 4:25 AM
To change pillowcases, empty ashtrays and pick up blankets
We are small, brown-skinned, with curly hair
Colombo by night
We don't wear panties to dance on bar tables
We hold brooms
We hold vacuum cleaners
We have thin chests, short legs, and hair held in buns
Song of Ceylon
O Robert Flaherty
We don't have gold nose rings

    First woman: I have a child at home
        Who's sleeping with his father
        His father works during the day
    Second woman: I have two children at home
        Who are sleeping with their paternal
          grandmother
        Their father is a laborer overseas
    Third woman: I have three children at home
        Who are sleeping with each other
        I don't know where their father is
        Whether in the Army or with a lover

We don't greet the nodding passengers
Traveling from Singapore to Dubai
They are going from the Philippines to Oman to build
From Thailand to Abu Dhabi to clean and sweep
From Indonesia to Kuwait to babysit and raise chickens
    (I take care of other people's children
    But when I go home on leave
    I'll buy for my own child a computer
      game as a present)
    (And I'm saving money to get married)
    (And I'm working to pay off debts)
On the United Arab Emirates airliner they are nodding off to sleep
Sleep well all you long distance laboring heroes
We also don't greet the air stewardess
From England Finland Denmark and Egypt (with dyed blond hair)
We do not greet them
We are the laborers from Ceylon
Boarding the airplane before dawn
We walk on the runway carrying trash bags.

Do Kh.

TRAN TIEN DUNG was born in Go Cong in 1958 and now lives in Ho Chi Minh City. He is the author of four books of poetry, *Moving Mass* (1997), *Appear* (2000), *Chicken Feather Duck Feather Sky* (2003) and *Two Flowers On The Forehead Of A Second Class Citizen* (2006). His poems have been translated into English by Linh Dinh, and published in *Manoa*. "Monologuist with Light Pole on Bolsa Avenue" was written after a visit to Orange County in May of 2007, during his first trip to the US.

At The Barbershop

Me, if I look into the barbershop mirror I want to be a revolutionary   it's
not clear, between hairstyles and the art of cleaning out ear wax, which is a
more satisfying revolution. I am a dark-skinned, working class man, and don't
normally pay attention to that value, but if someone pastes the color red or
white on my eyes, I go crazy immediately   my entire body darkens into the
color of blood pudding mixed with the aroma of mint leaves and peanuts. I
hate to join the uprising of those at wine bar but each evening I'm drowned in
that piss smell. I crave the sort of wine brewed from the sea   the sea speaks
a universal language   the sea cuts hair and cleans out earwax several times
a month   each clump of hair   each clump of earwax   is a ship carrying
consciousness of democracy to help shriveled old men become boys with large
foreheads incubating dreams of becoming the president.

Tran Tien Dung

Chicken-Feather-Duck-Feather Sky

Chicken-feather-duck-feather sky   a sneeze redolent of five spices. Schools over flames, one and all can learn about fear, the lessons dragging from one night to the next   each night fear is honed into a sword planted on a head a place where the wind howls. Fear! That's the kind of music I want to hear not always good but a safe kind of music. I listen to it endlessly   I listen until death and the criminal just want to return the corpses.

The Out-of-Breath Cove

to Linh Dinh

1

He thinks, watches his thought, waits for the thought to escape from the bottomless pit. He says to a school of thoughts swimming with their mouths wide open in the out-of-breath cove: You guys' survival is dependent on the life of a metal strip the kind with two sharp points to poke into hearts stab rocks.

He quaffs a sound   I listen   he sings

A drizzle
The deaf lady runs into the house the old lady falls into the river

Each day he wears a hat and shields his mouth from the light. He takes his voice to the river. There are millions of old ladies sitting inside the shrine, millions of old ladies sucking their voices like betel leaves and spitting out bruised red voices at the silent sky.

He swallows audibly, opens his mouth so the obscene melody from youth can be puffed out one sound at a time, jumping after bullfrogs and flowing into a hysterical rain. Everything has lost its haven.

2

When our family moved to this village, I forced my daughter to go the voice-supermarket. She was three.

A girl her age used the voice of a spat-out gum to smear my daughter's face, another used a strange voice to yank her pants down to check the brand of her underwear, another time a can of fruit spat its voice into her eyes, so that her vision now has a dull yellow color.

I worry about the fate of my daughter. I follow her closely whenever she goes out to prevent her from retaliating with that sort of voice. I'm in danger of having the other children's mothers swallow my head whole. In this village people can quickly become tense, to live each day they have to swallow and spit out a horribly heavy sound, even a slight reaction may cause one to be knocked dead. You say I should be careful, thank you! I cannot, I desire to live correctly, my objective is to soon determine the shape of this village's voice.

Monologuist with Light Pole on Bolsa Avenue

He stands on Bolsa Avenue with the yellow light poles
each light pole a friend of the exile,
he came here with only yellow as a friend
a tall and wide yellow.
Each day he looks up and says
"I'll go home early to cook up a pot of rice.
perhaps today we'll escape from the liquor's shadow."

"A part of this land truly belongs to the yellow
of cow piss and scorched clumps of grass,
there are too many pieces of beef dying inside the mouth,
a piece of American cowhide creating a bitter yellow glow."

Each day he looks up and says

"But how come I
don't belong anywhere
the color of beef fat in the pho restaurant Hạnh
                          the color of music in the Ly Ly café
nothing but the American color both delicious and tedious.
Each morning I step out of a dream
Shriveled and dry,
the telephone cannot call that woman
only a call to yellow.
Each night I step into the liquor's fume
my drunken voice at night cannot call the hooker,
I can only talk with yellow and
after a very long story
yellow spreads again a thick blanket on Bolsa Avenue."

"I used to imagine a strange yellow,
in other word I used to believe yellow was a pair of wings
a pair of wings originating from a torment in the East
a pair of wings as sunlight soothing so much sadness
but why do I still look up.
Torment and sadness cannot rub out fear.
I fear the smell of Communism, I fear the smell of American butter."

"I stand here next to a light pole on Bolsa Avenue
spread my arms wide like an eagle,
there's no America eagle with the color of chicken feathers.

I still look up.
I still love the chickens I've accidently squeezed to death and still
                              mourn the fate of chicks.
I still love yellow blood already dry and that bewildered soul."

"I still look up there.
There's no America eagle with the color of chicken feathers.
I fear the American color, I fear the color of Communism."

"I stand here on Bolsa Avenue from day until night,
with no illusion
                    beyond the American system
                         beyond the Communist hunt.
My fear sees through everything but the color of the sea."

"I came here from the sea.
The sea is a monster is a pair of free wings.
I stand here with the Bolsa light poles
fearing the place of refuge the place escaped from.
I stand inside the sea dawn
facing an everlasting fear."

INRASARA was born in Ninh Thuan in 1957 and now lives in Ho Chi Minh City. He is the author of five volumes of poems and many scholarly books on the language and literature of Champa, a mostly Muslim, previously Hindu population. He is the only well-known poet of Champa descent, one of 54 minority groups in Vietnam, his work raising many issues not previously addressed in the Vietnamese context. As an essayist on contemporary Vietnamese poetry, Inrasara has discussed and praised many poets purposely ignored by the official media. He also writes poems in Champa, some of which are posted on his very active blog. His first novel, *Sand Portrait*, was published in 2006. In an interview, he said: "I've had all sorts of jobs: rice farming, growing grapes, running a coffee shop, petty commerce, veterinary, teaching…As for literature, I've also been involved in different fields […] It's not a problem! To switch activities is a useful way to take a break. It adds to your life experiences, enriches your language."

Allegory of the Land

I

Many friends have chastised me for wasting time on the Champa language
how many can read it? Who will remember it?
but I want to squander my entire life serving it
even if there're only half a dozen people
                even if there's only one
                        or no one!

II

A proverb—a line of folk poetry
half a children's song—a page of ancient poetry
I find and pick up
like a child a tiny pebble
(pebbles that adults carelessly step over)
to build a castle just for me to live in
a castle they'll need someday to shelter from the rain—I'm certain!

III

Flowers give off fragrance
no one smells—flowers emit into the wind
birds sing songs
no one hears—songs that fly all over the air
my soul reveals its gift
but you won't accept it—my sentiment rots.

IV

Purple flowers bloomed on my childhood knoll
the forest's gone
bald and desolate knoll
just for me perhaps this solitary evening
the bare branches are still trying to bud.

V

Like a look backward of a son going to war
        after building a home for his aging mother
like a look backward of a true monk
        after building a temple for true believers
an itinerant field worker
hit the road while looking back at the tender rice stalks blooming

VI
What did ocean say to shore, as shore cuddled ocean?
thank you generous shore for your open arms
what did bee say to flower, as flower gave bee its stamen?
thank you flower for your bounty
what did tree say to earth, as tree gave shade to earth?
thanks for teaching me about receiving
and us
what do we say to each other, as we give each other hands, lips and glances?
what will I say to you?
what will you say to me?

VII
A growth of young trees eagerly sprouting on the moor
but their roots are not deep in the earth
only one storm is needed
to rip them up.

VIII
The old sunny hill's deserted
the buffalo bell has stopped clacking
where's the forest for buffalos to get lost in?
wearing the bell the buffalo scowled
now the road's blank and smooth
remember the bell—the buffalo's sad.

IX
Her skin somewhat pale—she denied she was Champa
a few months overseas—he didn't admit to being Vietnamese
out of self-respect—Karl Jaspers didn't consider himself German
Henry Miller rejected America—because of his hatred of war
there is a huge gap between not admitting and rejecting.

X
A flashing glimpse from the father
half a smile from the mother
and your two distant hands
among the vastness of our native sunshine
are asking me where else can one find heaven?

TRAN WU KHANG is the author of 16 poems and 5 essays on <tienve.org>. Inrasara wrote about him: "Tran Wu Khang is an amateur writer, with a few articles published around 1996. He disappeared for nearly a decade, then resurfaced in 2004. In my opinion, he has made three contributions worth noticing: 1) two pretty good poems, "Gift of the Devil" and "The Griefs of Criticism" 2) the essay "The Professional Amateur Critic" and especially 3) some essays that triggered discussions about younger poets." Many people, myself included, believe that Tran Wu Khang is no other than Inrasara.

Gift of the Devil

poets make poems—I terrorize
boys and girls make out—I terrorize
seamstresses enter factories, kids leave schools—I terrorize
they gamble—I terrorize
they bath in the ocean—I terrorize
they panic, they're injured, they die—
I terrorize churches, governments, hotels, markets, mad houses, subways
sunny, rainy, windy, stormy, traffic jams, the dollar fluctuates—I terrorize
priests give sermons, singers barhop, the ruling class oppresses, billionaires bilk
funds, the poor starve—I terrorize

they make love
they procreate
they raise and educate each other
they praise or condemn each other
they deceive or are frank with each other
they worry about AIDS the black hole the green revolution the white death
I terrorize

no one terrorizes—I terrorize
it doesn't matter if any person, group or party terrorizes or not—I terrorize
I admit to being a terrorist, whether or not it was me who terrorized
they protest and condemn me—I terrorize

mankind globalize or return to the caves—I still terrorize
I terrorize on earth, the moon, mars, the comets, I terrorize everywhere
on stars they'll discover millions of years from now
dead in this life I'll continue to terrorize into infinity in subsequent lives

happy—I terrorize; sad—I terrorize; neither happy nor sad—I terrorize
I eat sleep fuck piss just to terrorize
they make bombs, I buy—I terrorize
unable to buy, I make my own—I terrorize

TERRORIST is MY name
it's what I do, it's my fate, my love and hate, my game and war, my promised
land, my reality and void, my belief and passion, my heaven...
I terrorize I terrorize I terrorize
terrorize terrorize terrorize

voices

birdschirping   singing

singing   birdschirping

                    TERRORISM

criesforhelp   begging

begging   criesforhelp

                    sobbing

                    I TERRORIZE
                    I TERROR
                    I TERR
                    I T
                    I
                    .

NGUYEN QUOC CHANH was born in 1958 in Bac Lieu, and now lives in Ho Chi Minh City. He is the author of four collections of poems, *Night of the Rising Sun* (1990) and *Inanimate Weather* (1997), the e-book *Coded Personal Info* (2001) and the samizdat *Hey, I'm Here* (2005). In 2001, he published a translation of T.S. Eliot's "The Waste Land." His poems have been translated into English by Linh Dinh and printed in *The Literary Review, Filling Station, Sibila, Almost Island, Of Vietnam: Identities in Dialogue* (Palgrave 2001) and *Three Vietnamese Poets* (Tinfish 2001). In 2005, he was invited by the Haus der Kulturen der Welt to give a reading in Berlin. Chanh's poems are raw, wild, deft and bitterly funny. The backbone of the Saigon scene, he is also widely admired for his fearless political stance.

Seven Untitled Poems

The sun lunges forward crossing a boundary puncturing a late sleep.
An egg hatches a sound.
I grip my own hand holding a shadow and releasing it into a glass of water.
On the silent shore the sea of memories spares two shells odorless and empty.

*

Evening holding back a burnt mark a pictogram the pit of an eye the sun immolated,
Evening burning the memory bank arms held in prayer the night heron calling into
space,
Night extinguished with one man left behind lunging forward turning into a
shadow...
Evening Who?

*

Feet without lamp street without lamp the shadow is black.
Feet without lamp street with lamp black is the shadow.
Beneath two lamps two shadows both are black.

*

You ran contrariwise from the crown of your head to the soles of your feet, a mad
woman, a primitive egg dashed against scrap metal.
You collided then reverted to a rubbery condition a series of warped circles.
The endlessly jarring road with its bad intentioned collisions and drowned rivers.
You ran in panic from the woods onto a tidy stage then smiled and talked in a
bisexual manner.
Beneath the conceptual hammer you boldly split in two rhythmically trembling on
the resilient mattress.
You chased after a fit of excess and fell into the HIV pit.
A strange wind poured into the fire.
You a gray smoke gathering into clouds metamorphosing into a female bug like
the woman in the dunes adapting to a man robbed of freedom without his
day on the cross.
You a woman about to be stoned.

*

My eyes do not register the presence of trees animals men or even the arrogant
horizon.
Inside my eyes are only distances hierarchies dark holes black boxes zigzags and
Disquiets.

*

Daybreak frolics with the flowers the night smile disappearing on the street.
Each person a curfew face inside the clock the pendulum oscillates.
The briefest day I throw away as you save the thin pleasured body.
Daybreak swallows you in stages nibbles me to bits.

*

Tic toc tic toc
The horn beak pecks at the night drum,
Two secret revealing eyes are sliding along time's greasy surface.
The wall displays dead holes variously connected to the inmate.
And only the tic toc sounds remain to count the rolling aspirins.
Night flashes its cold teeth the mouth opens its precipices.
Shadows from cul-de-sacs stretch and stagnate on the brick floor.
Still the tic toc sounds pecking the dense night.
Still the rolling aspirins.

Low Pressure System

The thumb stops breathing.
There is a sound of a dropped glass.
Needles piercing the ear.

I see water gushing from hollows in the wall.
(The house's arterie is broken.)

Water is drowning the word mouth.
A character cannot escape the death of a wet book.
Our character is tattooed: Small. Weak. Wicked. Shell.

Words stepping on each other trying to remove themselves from literariness.
They float blue on the water.
Individual corpses sink to compete with bricks and shards of glass.

The remaining fingers have headaches and runny noses.
Memory stands then sits stringing pieces of intestines around a hole.

I hear cries of a newborn.
A fish crawls out from a bloody hollow.
The woman closes her thighs and a corpse is covered up.

A laugh wiggles across a cheek.
Look into the thumb.
Sperms reborn in flowing sap animating wild grass and flowers.

After the bee season flowers and grass are plowed up shredded and burnt.
Grass regrows and the sperms open their eyes.
(Even if the land is mortgaged joint ventured or sold to another.)

The hunt is a thousand years old.
A distance only blind eyes can perceive.
Its concentrated flavor cannot be tasted by anyone besides the moss covered
tongues of turtles.

I hear wild laughs from a circus mixed with the rhythmic prayer for the release of
the souls of many female nuns.
(They are performing a circus for another world?)

A low pressure system on the hill seeps into the body.

Termites dig up dirt inside bones.
Nests grow from the ground to resemble artistic graves.

I carry a cemetery inside my body.
A fist missing a finger.

Marsh Dream

I

Broken fuse. Night unfurled from objects oozes out misplaced eyes and all are infected.
Taut threads on the face of criminal justice leaches heat loses abilities to ejaculate.
As for the sacred spot, it is glazed over with a spreading yellow film and spills onto the
demarcation line rams against the forbidden zone.
Annoying eye. Sedimentary mouth sucks on pride a soapberry lava ceases at the border of real and fake weathers.
Spent senses. Life stops flowing. Everything rots into fragments only the echoes of a linga and yoni unperturbed statues still gloomily reverberating…

II

Broken fuse. Things declare themselves royalties. The faithful let down their guards.
It's a legal chance for a disorderly appearance. Order is restored by a red malice.
An inflected voice suffers rising blood pressure dreams of nux vomica and empty wine bottles.
The cerebrum enacts a theatrical wholly feminine.
The hand of monopoly nudges the god-given rights of living things. Skin color loses its reflex and the spool of the past weaves a fabric to cover holes too tiny to pass on the ambition to increase air-hating insects.
Staring eyes lose the key to open and shut at will.
Obnoxious air. Manikins dementedly slack. Each manikin hides a pig's tail in Macondo (the village in One Hundred Years of Solitude) and animal-shaped clouds jump on each other's backs without   distinguishing between predators and preys lions rabbits cats dogs or   horses…
The humilated being opens its door. The pressures of surpluses and deficits ooze out beyond the range of sight and sense and accent marks.
The face of lava is not in the book of divination. The protuberance is sharp and pliable.
The hollow has a black hole element its shape changes according to the weather of a half yawn.

III

Broken fuse. Night smoothes out protuberances and fills in hollows. Disparity aches the entire back of the head and windpipe fills in tail bone pelvis bone and an open toilet. The savior sits.
Concepts are a constraining helmet insects catching prey by a system of tight enclosure.
Imagination eternally malnourished. A thick shadowed man does not hear the air break disturbing the road to the cemetery.
Look into one spot. Staring and contemplating is to enter a train car without passengers.
Imagination thrown into a blinding interval everything rises. A straight movement eliminates dampness and dries out the viscera.
The hammock shadow swings creakily. The sound of darkness moving darkened by slime. Kinship swells made visible through hastily carved bas relief where air-hating insects worship.
Gnawing epoch. Suck marrow. Product of forced cohabitation and of the instinct to pressure a young forest.
A curt hand. Memory opens its aperture and train cars without passengers.
The past has superfluous tickets. Centuries not transported.

IV

Broken fuse. A fluorescent screen from a dark corner displays in wiggly lines manikins from the century before silent films.
A vanguard manikin sticks out his slimy tongue dun colored stinking and oozing from intermittent cracks the conspiracies to infiltrate eternity.
No images no smells no nothing. Tipped equilibrium.
Insects compete to sing in chorus the swamp refrain. Rain is. Don't hide in the entrance. Outside still moving forward train cars carrying nothing.
Two oversized thigh bones incarcerating the desert. Dip everything into the dish-washing tub.
Eliminate the lead. Cover up the-system-to-prevent-fire-to-the-senses. The past is bonfires of memory an on duty death notice.
Two overlong ditties emit a haunting melody like a mumbled prayer.
A door opens. The secret spills out onto the street. Insects drone and crackle. The swamp sleeps deeply. Run, run and run...
A bottle filled with words. Dirty. An expressive hand over-pours the glass because rats and cockroaches have splashed onto the wall slanting shadows and squares.
Interred bricks.
A disquieting word strikes. Recovering viscera. Those of the same skin color emit timelessly.

Beefsteak

Cows are really the past.
Bulls were worshipped.

They seized meadows.
They taught each other how to marinate and dry with success.
They found amusement by inventing ways to ridicule cadavers.

(Dead things bred daily and took turns onto the throne for the sacred object.)

Cows continue to procreate and the ring has slipped.
Worm color replaces grass color.
From a purebred worm the cows maintain a throne under the auspice of the sacred
object religion.

Eyes that can only see what's behind.

From those eyes the cows procreate.
Also from those eyes the cows maintain the throne of the sacred object.
Also from those eyes the present has no more meadows.

The present is only cows consuming dishonest grass.

Their meat is starting to be displayed in supermarkets.
Their meat is bloodless and odorless.

They are preparing a beefsteak for an immortal deity.

Nguyen Quoc Chanh

Rap Music

Hands steadily spinning.
Guarding each number for a chance to shrink into one spot.

All things peeled.
Unchanging season.

Fading paint on furniture.
Bottles and scraps of paper not becoming garbage.
Accidents remaining at sites.
Pores not excreting.
Genitals neither generating nor receiving heat.

Population growth through test tubes.

An old monk chanting with his prayer beads on this play button.
A young embittered black man playing rap on that play button.
And on my play button a bass rhythm clogged up soggy without transmigration.

In the morning the Red Guard sperms are all blind.

They are bats facing the wall.
They are heads masturbating to the point of impotence.

And the squashed penis is lying and listening to rap.

A World Of Sand

The day lies face down on top of night, he and things
Sleep in deep pleasure. Time is many bats

Cutting the night's darkness into irregular bits, each bit
A live rhythm to splash into the crowd

And from this crowd, another empty space
Slams down the door. The room

Swells and flexes. Shuddering on leaving a runway, opening the body—
Two sympathetic systems mix heat through the night. On the day

The hedge collapses, he dreams fearful of aging, let
The shadow flows and suddenly, all shapes

Are identical. He and blocks of monochromatic
Colors cover the wall, play the morning game

Of an imagination avoiding shapes, evicting all things from their spoken names,
A figure is dropped into a bottomless sensation... Have intercourse

With savages. With the sheep Dolly, a mountain peak capable
Of getting horny rides another, sculpts symbols

Of debauchery without shape and impression, and
Manifesting predictions of balance

In a divination book. As a prediction of imbalance, he
Can only survive by expelling the sadness of teeth and hair,

The sadness of sap oozing. As a stutterer
In a world crisscrossed with directives, and in a wretched

Coincidence, he becomes lost in a deluge.
(The seasons supplant each other, until the season of

Disintegration.) A sun ray crosses through, he hears it
Reverberating in his blood. He longs to wraps his arms

Around a cow's neck and to frolic with children. He carries
A fresh fear, the fear of a woman imprisoned

Nguyen Quoc Chanh

Inside the birth mark of menopause, turning back
To a lost stretch of the road, counting fallen eggs on top of the vault

Of the thirtieth. A night of the alphabet, of intonations,
Of the flowering hour, of white enthusiasm. And the breasts

Of the earth are always shifting into puberty, so the well-worn roads
Will grow lush, and the body will retreat into the swamp reeds, and memory

Will detach itself from all things. Drop a thought into water
To reach a world of sand...

Revolving Stage

I

The spine twists, wraps the sea swallow into the eye. The stage spread its legs and spins. A light remaining from puberty plucks a woman from someone else's look.

Mixed among the pebbles, an eye says: "Owls fly out from the vagina." A dog runs after a bone's caress. "Let's keep it," a hand reaches out.

A burning smell in last night's dream. The morning is stuck in a calcium-deficient yawn of a mandible. A finger lets go of faith. A complicated emotion fans out. A blue fly bends down into the pit of a bottle inside the trash can of repentance.

I dream of a one stringed violin. The past stores up a fishy smell. The sudden death image of a bird in flight. Hundreds of terracotta masks drop. The electric fan is addicted to the wind. An old thought is remade by a set of false teeth.

Swimming inside an intestine, a man drowning in words chase after the phrase: "Savage homes."A crippled child from the Central region selling lottery tickets says morosely: "Mrs. Huyen goes up the Tranverse pass on a Minsk motorcycle sitting behind a driver with artificial hands." Beer bottles snap their caps and scream excitedly; 1,2,3... go. Idiocy ferments and foams.

Growing from the asshole a herd of traditional domestic animals, vines with soft thorns climb a metal fence of a viscous city with a million inhabitants afflicted with night blindness. A history of shadows does not believe in words. A damp poet makes poetry with images.

A morning excercise with six breaths for one movement. On a bed Without Character, a light metal ring left behind by a little Chinese circus girl.

Shimmering satellite disks sending and receiving signals. From an empty bottle. From an old book. From a rotten tooth. From a fish dead from the drought. From prayer beads. From an obscenity. A string of monosyllabic news tumbles from the vocabulary of run-on sentences.

A cat catches an elephant and puts him inside a bamboo basket. Neither sadness nor happiness exist. An awareness of indigestion towards dying without even a haircut. Water leaks from the sense to the root of a hair of a stuffed animal standing in the Straw Warrior Square.

Night with the blue of early summer weather. A fading woman, the seasoned face of a tropical fish having had intercourse with a 110-volt light gives birth to a dance/theater/underwater palace tune causing a funhouse effect to retarded children.

A listless eye behind an urn. Incense sticks jostling each other to play the fog game. Fireflies on a dry branch sprinkle flames on dead leaves. A snail meets disaster on the North-South rail line. The tropics scoops out a deep cave. A fistful of mildew faces a Coke logo.

Inside a dirty shoe, toes breathe with difficulty. Carbon dioxide rhythm from the past smothers. A book opens, words decompose. An attentive look yields no meanings. Inside a thought: a short woman, continuously shaking bright colored rings.

In the year 2544 of the Buddhist calendar, two lizards intertwine on the Goddess of Mercy's stomach. A kid plays with insect noises made by an organ. My child is afraid her teeth are yellowing. I gargle three times a day with Listerine. Rent is going up.

The man who collects human bones says: "A Black person cannot become more black by humping up. A White person cannot become more white by arching his back. A Yellow person cannot become more yellow by doubling over. A Red person cannot become more red by going under."

A painting renounces colors on its own but the eye at the museum still retains them. A dog from a poor household barks into a daydream the white spots on a cat's back inside an empty house. The Blue Flagged King points his ass upwards and with his hands together dreams of traffic. Female Gust Number 7 finishes first at Phu Tho racecourse. Huynh Phan Anh loses forever one third of a blue ticket.

When eyes are shut any sound is white. Last night's dream hasn't escaped from the smell of dirty shoes. Down in the valley a herder raises his artificial leg to menace the past.

War of the genitals is replaced by a synthesized plastic. Music without windows. On the festival of death, bombed women inflate into enormous wombs, become sources of brutal bloodlines.

Land of the museum holding evidences of oddly shaped life forms. The reptant strength of a damp culture, and the homosexuals like to tattoo onto the generative organ images of bugs and venomous creatures.

Nightly news of a low pressure system, and flood, overflow the TV stations. A belief from the river's source shatters dykes packed with pasty earth lumpy inside heads falling asleep.

The ancestors are underwater. Faith and filial piety wait for emergency food. The ghosts are demanding Miliket instant noodles. The kinds of death not found in dictionaries, and life shits and pisses on concepts.

Drowsy eyes wait for sleep. There is a man who has been hanged from a roof. A death with the beauty of a small waterfall pouring down from a jagged peak. A comedy performed by an old monkey. His image has been printed on postcards to sell to tourists.

Death has no gender. The entire body is bound with musical strings. Testimonies are taped all over the hallway. A few words clump their heads together, ancient characters hobnobbing with complicated constructions erected by absent minded individuals. The grammar of those who believe that, after a night's sleep, they will wake up mute.

Among green and red signals, streets coagulate. At the intersection of Great Humongous Vietnam Plaza, a project gives its death notice. Next to a pile of broken bricks: garbage, animal carcasses and strewn humanity.

A horn shrieks. The crowd surges, screaming: "Kill! Kill! Kill!" A saxophone soloist suffers a stroke in the middle of Castaways. The stage turns 180 degrees. The MC smiles, apologizes for the technical glitch. A jazz singer sings Spring On The Steps, ass swaying, breasts heaving.

Reason for the accident is determined by the sharp nose of a rabid dog.

Wide Open Eye

A day of dark glasses
(Detective eyes look into a crevice.)

The ocean surface calm, to hear sunken ships break apart.

Bodies rot inside the memory of wide-open eyes.

Centuries of typhoons, the sunken ships become ghostly waves, become voices
of matchsticks.

To light a candle for cold fingers.
(The candle flame wipes clean a secret smudge.)

Only the wind knows of sea birds sinking and dissolving inside wide-open eyes.

And ships with sounds not spotted with rust.

Adventures stored inside children's dreams.
(Dream swells into a burden a sudden accident.)

A beauty only time is violent enough to be indicted.

And all the judges will be children, (and all will be acquitted.)

A Legend

A vacation on top of a stove.
Smoke preserves the shoots.
Warmth maintains the timbres.

The seed I store inside the tropical forest's vagina.
A woman born from a fever and two eyes not gouged out by the color yellow.
They are reminiscences soundly asleep inside a legendary skirt.

Every situation in the story has cats, rabbits and some fruits.
Besides the sounds of cats and dogs, there are also cormorants, guavas,
mangoes, and a bottle of fish sauce.

One among them said if stuck on a desert island he would only need: Mozart
and fish sauce.

I am a bear who does not know how to dance on stilts and juggle seven swords,
only lucky to survive the uprooted forest.
I was born from a tree's hollow and my umbilical cord was cut with a potsherd
and my music is that of a woodpecker.
My smell is that of the saliva of bees mating with the honey of flowers.
My road is to climb to the trifurcated crotch of a tree to be full and drunk and
to ponder for a moment then letting go and falling down.

After each fall my flesh becomes elastic and expands.
After each fall my plants grow boundlessly.
After each fall my animals multiply.
I'm tattered, I'm porous, I'm smooth, I'm bitter. And I'm...

Although I'm only an uninsured seed and without wings.

In a dense instance of idle bullets, I take off and land.

In the legend I'm the survivor who has seen the head at the bottom of a jar of
fermented paste.

Chopping Down Trees to Plant Humans

Punished, a student must fill two sheets: I won't stir.
Punished, a student must slap himself: 56 times.
Punished, a student is forbidden to fart: for a month.
Punished, a student is banned from bleeding: during her period.
Punished, a student must drink salt water: for being rude during morality class.
Punished, a student must swallow his report card: grades below average.
Punished, a student must sit in the toilet and sing the national anthem: for
buckling his knees during the national anthem.
Punished, a student must yank a thousand itchy hairs from the Principal's head:
for scratching his head, yawning and not being able to distinguish between
dinosaurs and reptiles.
Punished, a student must smear soot on his classmate's forehead: for not helping
his friend keep quiet.
Punished, a student must suck an eraser during history class: for not
remembering all 800 names of our heroes.
Punished, a student must shut his eyes for a week for not memorizing the poem:
Tonight Uncle Ho Doesn't Sleep.

12 years later there's a student who goes limp down there.
12 years later there's a student with his left cheek puffier than his right.
12 years later there's a student addicted to foul smells.
12 years later there's a student with an ovariectomy.
12 years later there's a student with a broken larynx.
12 years later there's a student who tears each piece of paper he sees.
12 years later there's a student who doesn't dare to shit in a toilet.
12 years later there's a student who yanks everyone's hair.
12 years later there's a student who often grabs rice from other people's bowls.
12 years later there's a student who must piss at the sight of a statue.
12 years later there's a student who converts to islam to look for Saddam's bones.

More than 20 years ago I was a student who could never stand straight.
Now I own a utility pole 25 meter-high though I can't steer my bladder.

Disconnected Thoughts

Kids are twigs, schools an *animal farm*, my son's overstuffed memory a clam shell cracking open, and what's more: life dissolves inside a beautiful shell.

Saigon punctured, a corpse not yet buried, the capital sinks a few inches each day, politics should also be equitized.

Alchemy's parasite is a cluster of fly-infested words waiting for the train at the Temple of Literature station, all the beggars a game for the release of the soul: the posthumous text spears and disembowels the reader.

Exhume the rubber band past, restore the gecko color, a trouser bottom ridicules a heel: Rising Dragon* becomes a dirt dragon.

Spring poetry day, swallowed whole, a public stomach, a revival of the field rat aesthetic: soon the day to repay the revolution.

The heritage's legs are tired, the intinerant noodle-peddling child disappears inside his clacking, the tradition of burying cajuput stakes to raise a tall house: clueless aesthetics the offspring of cruelty.

Smart war, to convert every form of peace into presumptuousness, the fake dog meat crowd loses an ally: why are there people fearful of peaceful changes?

The beach loses electricity, a school of slick skinned fish with oil spilling into gills, it's impossible to drape Romantism onto waves: Gia Long** gives a snake a piggy back ride, Ho Chi Minh bites the house chicken.

The cai luong*** opera boat sinks, a civil war between fleas and cockchafers, North Korea improves the secretions of the Vietnamese Revolution Museum: Ho Chi Minh City should move to Nghe An****.

An attacking tactic forces the insolent reading method into the void, inside a garden a hen gains weight, Pham Duy***** waits for *The Nation to Repent* and Nhat Linh****** died more beautifully than a writer should.

Confused is the fertile fate of the bronze drum intonation, words survive thanks to crossbreeding.

Lofty aesthetics imported from Russia, to convert shiftiness into a madam abusing the library.

Now art is a fake 50,000 dong bill, used at the supermarket without detection, words self neuter.

A mountain goat on snowy mountain swallows saliva, cloud flows into mouth.

A punished child is made to eat again what he's thrown up, yet at home he waits a long time before telling his mom.

A poet searches a public trash can to approximate a type of bird dead with its beak wide open polluted by a handful of inspirations, still he can't stand firm.

National secrets are feasts derived from the fortunes of poppies, to be human is to be humiliated, to be Vietnamese is to be super humiliated.

The abused child will grow up fully nourished by a cradle hatred, his memory infected by a garlic stink.

Language taken hostage, a stick needed to start the morning exercise, the dirtiest word is revolution,

Someone advertises on the Web: I need a sexual partner who's a vangard in thoughts and actions.

Metaphysical philosophers are meteors who don't cause marshland residents to feel aches and pains, and "intellectual" here is the toilet paper.

Infinity sometimes extends only from thumb to pinkie, the body is eroded.

A tantric buddhist says: the evil inside the pyramid is the cause of 9/11 there's no danger.

A six-year-old kid wants to kill his mom if she doesn't hurry up and buys his teachers presents for the terrifying Teachers' Day.

From a mess of bones just found on a Truong Son mountain trail, a few candies still intact between scorched crotch bones.

If reincarnated Karl Marx would say: Microsoft is the new opium industry.

Behind the lice monument, history spreads out a mess of civil wars, the Vietnamese dictionary hasn't define the phrase overseas escape.

Occasionally even a bed can upset a person, and one's insomnia seldomly balances out another's oversleeping.

Coco York Africanizes after midnight listeners who have not taken a sleeping pill.

Pleasure is the nabbing of images from the imagination of someone swimming against the current, because the river's source is the sewer.

To protect himself from the acceleration of the red letter crowd, a poet has turned a bottle into a lover with huge breasts.

Translator's notes:
*Rising Dragon, Thăng Long, was the name of Hanoi, in use from 1010 until 1788.
**Gia Long (1762-1820) was an emperor whose reliance on French advisors lead to France's eventual occupation of Vietnam.
***cai luong is a modern form of folk opera
****Nghệ An is Ho Chi Minh's birthplace.
*****Vietnam's foremost song composer. He was born in Hanoi in 1921, lived in Saigon from 1951 until 1975, the US from 1975 until 2005, where he returned to Saigon to live. *The Nation Repents,* a book by France-based Nguyen Gia Kieng, is an in-depth examination of flaws in the Vietnamese character.
******Nhat Linh (1905-1963) was a pioneer of Vietnamese fiction. He committed suicide to protest the Ngo Dinh Diem government, the same year that Thich Quang Duc immolated himself.

Three Poems

1.

I'm his daddy—
Although the broad who gave birth to him isn't my wife.

He calls me father—
Although I'm not older than him.

I gave him a name,
And I can withdraw it as I wish.

I gave him a domain,
Yet I'll chew him out should he approach that spot.

I don't consider him a dog,
So why does he bark when I eat dog meat?

Is he trying to act like a bastard here?
Don't think the glorious era of feudalism is over!

2.

He has one head but four shadows even.
Three fourths of what's in his head is liquid.
He scorns the head but reveres the shadows.
He is digusted by solids and craves liquids.
He stores the head in a plastic bag.
He dangles the shadows in his room.
He strikes the head and strokes the shadows.
He's been doing that for thirty years.

The head is all liquid now.
The head is now afraid of the shadows.
The head is all liquid now.
The shadows are his virtual destiny.

3.

He cups the dry corpse's ass with two hands.
He scrubs the feeble body with two hands.
He belabors his prick also with two hands.

But he squeezes that deep-yellow poet's breast with his right hand.
But he rubs that pitch-black prose writer's head with his left hand.
But in front of that redder than red idealogue he folds his arms.
Downing bottles, he recites furiously: *Our hands are capable of everything...*

Post, Post, but not Post...

Straight on: my face's blank.
Aslant: my face's askew.
Below or above: my face's equally messed up.

Next to a Cambodian: I'm gloriously yellow.
Next to a Westerner: I flatten myself in panic.
Next to a Chinese. I timidly squint.

Previous life: my core was monkey.
This life: my community is ghostly.
Next life: my country a commune.

Past: I tattooed myself, fought the Chinese.
Now: my granddad hawks tofu.

Past: I flexed myself against the French.
Now: my dad mends shoes on the sidewalk.

A while ago: I risked my life against the Americans.
Now: my wife is anxious to marry an American.

Sometimes I want to forget: O the ones who cry alone!
Sometimes I want to believe: O the ones who cry alone!
Sometimes I want to go mad: O the ones who cry alone!

(To the Supreme Ho, Nong and sundry comrades)

They blather that I fool around to renew my prick. They mock that my wife has left me clearly a lame prick. They mumur that I'm with this and that broad a whorish prick. They rumor that I tussle with the enemy without being arrested likely an undercover prick. They see that I've fucked a skull open so they yell there's a terrorist prick. They slander that I laugh out loud while outraged surely a psycho prick. Poking they see that I don't perform (confidence) tricks so they shout he's a humorless prick. They gather tidbits then sneer as they teach me how to make my prick perform. Prick is not just a word meaning limp or hard, but its contents are also the straight forward secretion of what cannot be indifferent towards the obscene counterfeiting of the intellect, arts, politics and morals. Prick morality must be a hard prick after a cunt is aroused. Yet political prick is a limp prick after China threatened to become aroused. Yet artistic prick is an aroused prick in tandem with the aroused public. Yet intellectual prick is a prick swinging its main organ from limpness to arousal. And tomorrow there's yet another aroused demonstration. When the Chinese Communist Party prick is hard the Vietnamese Communist Party prick is limp. Because both parties belong to the same nutsack.

December 15, 2007

TRINH THANH THUY was born in Saigon and lives in southern California. Her poetry is included in the anthology *Between L and C* (California, 2001). She has published essays and poems in many web and print journals, including *Tien Ve, Talawas* and *Hop Luu,* her critical take on contemporary Vietnamese poetry particularly sweeping and astute.

On Fuji's Summit

Forest ceases breathing
awake
chirping bird sounds
conscious
soothing mountain air
frolicking prayer flags flying
Japan purples self chaotic ink strokes
pine shapes stacking green towards the day's feet even
house row curving waist hugging unsnuffed lanterns
bitter drop green tea
goose down quilt faintly snags a human scent
a hair left behind pillow bound
a hair still buzzed clinging to Fuji cloud ceiling
woman nude in mineral spring lake
evokes nature
hot breasts dazzle sun
feet escort earth spirit
a secret death
umbilical cord
yet sealed with samurai image

Bedroom Tales

Done, the first lover hugs her and falls asleep. In the middle of night, he complains of the heat, turns on the air conditioner, hugs a pillow and sleeps. Complaining of the cold, she gets up to turn off the air conditioner, hugs the blanket and sleeps. He turns it on, she turns it off, on off, off on, all night. In the morning, she says we're not compatible, let's not hang out anymore.

Done, the second lover hugs her and falls asleep. In the middle of the night, she wakes up to complain that he was snoring too loudly. He sleeps, she wakes, she wakes, he sleeps. All night, she hugs the blanket and pillow, twisting and turning. In the morning, she grabs blanket and pillow, takes off without even saying sayonara.

Done, the third lover hugs her and falls asleep. In the middle of the night, he gets up to turn off the fan, hugs blanket and sleeps. She complains of the heat, gets up, turns on the fan, hugs pillow and sleeps. He turns off, she turns on, off on, on off. In the morning, he says we're not compatible, let's split.

Living alone she hugs blanket and pillow and sleeps by herself.

Pig Valve

"Your heart valve must be replaced, otherwise you'll die," the surgeon asserts. "Is there no other way, doctor?" "We'll need to replace it with a pig's heart valve," the second surgeon concludes. "Why a pig's heart valve, doctor? So horrible!" "Your heart valve is defective and can only be fixed with a pig valve," the third surgeon decides. "I don't want to use a pig valve, I love animals, I can't consent to killing a life to save a life. I love plants. Let's replace my heart with a pine cone so I can smell its fresh resin moving along in my blood overflowing with life, can hear a pine exegesis rustling joyfully during evening prayer, can stand straight and tall during a turbulent storm. I love pines, love pines."

A year after the operation, the heart rejects the pig valve. She has a heart attack and passes away. Preparing her corpse they find in her vagina a young pine cone still lush and green.

Trinh Thanh Thuy   151

PHAN NHIEN HAO was born in 1967 in Kontum, Vietnam. He immigrated to the US in 1991 and now lives in Illinois. He has a BA in Vietnamese Literature from The Teachers College of Saigon, a BA in American Literature from UCLA, and a Master in Library Science, also from UCLA. He is the author of two collections of poems, *Paradise of Paper Bells* (1998) and *Manufacturing Poetry 99-04* (2004). His poems have been translated into English and published in the journals *The Literary Review, Manoa, xconnect* and *Filling Station*, and in *Of Vietnam: Identities in Dialogue* (Palgrave 2001), and in a full-length, bilingual collection, *Night, Fish and Charlie Parker*, the poetry of Phan Nhien Hao, translated by Linh Dinh (Tupelo 2006). For more on Phan Nhien Hao, see the interview in appendices.

Night Freedom

Geckos are frolicking in a yellow puddle
the street lamp an awakened eye
the night has buried deeply
the tedious hammering sounds of daily life
from the silence of the womb
a child is born
and the insane fellow will begin to bellow
about life floating through dangers
and humanity's fickleness
alienated from its five fingers
then fly upward during a blessed hour
upward
the yellow moon a ripe guava
the anguishing fruit of freedom of this ebony night
will be seeded tomorrow in the East.

Night's Dawn

Those are the invited secrets
in the middle of the night towards dawn
you tap the face of the clock with a hammer
the ceiling fan rotates beneath the moon
breathing in the smells of the city the way it was

There is another way to step out of
the blinding roars
of the poisonous night
but you rejected it
the ceiling fan and the flowers shed their petals
dawn repeats:
homicide
and a child eaten by dogs

There is another way to stop
halfway between two asphyxiations
but still you swim towards the sea
towards the secrets of the kelp.

Night, Fish and Charlie Parker

Night negotiating a plastic spoon
on a table littered with fish bones
all the illusions have been picked clean
Charlie Parker, a piece of bread not yet moldy
a black ocean and black notes
a few million years, a few small changes
at the bend in the road on the horizon
grows a strong type of tree
the black cat is in labor
gives birth to a few blue eggs.

Night in the South

A ringing phone on the carpet
a child is calling from the womb
night in the South
women open their doors to flirt
O spittle
the kind of germs belonging to wicked souls
returning to a cultured city
only to see ducks and chickens pecking on graves
shards of stars
encrusted in the deep dark horizon
the blue ocean and the monkish jellyfish
slackers are lining up
to buy cups of ice cream and a dripping night in the South
I walk on my hands
I drive 70 miles on the side of a mountain
the precipice is below
O the women, the jellyfish and the rosy cheeks
standing on the sidewalk with legs festively spread
all I have is jazz jazz jazz
                    and lots of gasoline in my bloody abyss.

Like the First Time

Like the first time I walked down the subway in New York
filthy and very fast
the train like a bullet shooting forward
from the barrel of busyness
a bright looking young man stood near the stairs singing:
"you are a small snake
curled around my neck
like green pearls from the sea
please don't kill me with your whispered poison"
I smiled and threw money into the paper cup,
the truth is I despise
everything having to do with snakes

Like the first time I was swallowed whole by my clothes
a serious suit worn for an interview
on the 48th floor of an ugly log-like building
in downtown Los Angeles
standing in the elevator I saw that I resembled a matchstick
struck against each day's dampness
in the process of making a living
I pushed the door open, walked in and saw
a heavy chested and large eyed secretary
and a brown coffee cup smeared with red lipstick
I said: "Ma'am, I am here to meet Jesus."

Like the first time I walked into a laundromat
to bleach out the lies
I ironed out sorrows and aromatized
the arrangements of fate and luck
faith in God can also be broadcast on TV
like a chase on the freeway
"breaking news," the announcer said,
"in the end the police had to shoot him
because of the danger he presented to others."

Phan Nhien Hao

The Black Haired Girl And I

I open the door and walk in
the black-haired girl disappears
at the last moment you will see her returning
to insult me
she is a small town secret
while I can read Latin

The two hands sewn into my pant pockets cannot be pulled out to wave
at a passing angel
an enormous butterfly with exaggerated genitals
she flies gently
pursued by an airplane
another butterfly made of steel
hairless and noisy

I recognize between East and West is a bicyclist
the black haired girl chasing the sun
you will see her returning
to insult me
she is a small town secret
while I can read Latin

But I am certain it will be a solar eclipse...

After Seven Days At A Hotel With T

I slept for seven days at a hotel with T
When I woke up I was a different person
I wanted to make money and I wanted to be a male bird
I wanted T to dive deep into my gullet
but she only swam back and forth like a fish
inside my mouth vault full of saliva

When I lay on T's body I thought I was paddling
a boat on sand
E LA NAVE VA
the sun was burning and our feet were buried
among worn out symbols
Ah, the sun is only a red stub
dying

Next to this woman I knew about hidden destruction
Like a person drinking endless cheap liquor
or an exhausted ropewalker who cannot sit down
normally I just cut the rope

There are too many things I cannot explain
the world is too small and conflicts are too great
I live alone near Hollywood
a nameless person among the faceless
I fight time and boredom with bouts of lovemaking

After seven days I walked out of the hotel with T
a bird in the sky suddenly grew tired
and dropped on my head like a rotten fruit
T said: it's nothing, only a case of mistaken identity
what time is it now H?
we need to go eat
The End.

Trivial Details

Inside an old car a heart sat behind the wheel
To circulate along the blood avenues
Where battles and a chaotic retreat occurred
In which my father was killed

I grazed her breasts and was wondering why she did not smile
It was what I had waited for all night inside a hut lit by a lantern
Her teeth resembled the keyboard of an unplugged organ

As a carpenter Christ should have made himself a coffin beforehand
Maybe that's only a trivial detail
But we live in a practical world and trivial details are often what generate beliefs

How to jump from the stove to the pan and back without tripping
My face is a doorknob
If you turn and enter, behind is a void I have to stock with stuff to convert into a
warehouse before sudden dusk

Wolves are sharing the corpse of a crow and hurling blood at the sky
There are fixed values and unnecessary rituals carried out because of instinctual
fear

"Ah, in the end He has come," the secretary says, bowing to the God of
miserable fates, then throws his ink pen at the gold fish inside the glass tank
That tiny world soon has the color of the sea
By doing so he becomes a creator

I watch a film with a telescope and imagine that I am from another planet
Who has abandoned his own kind a long time ago

A fat man kneels next to a woman who has just died
Says to take some of my flesh with you
Which you will need, when your own flesh has rotted
That is a dream I often see in my evening sleep

When bored and with some money I will travel
To a country where everything is coincidental
Man is born to be satisfied with waiting
Where I was born to wait for myself

The door slams with the sound of a vague collision from the other bank of the
river where fishermen are tapping their boats to chase fish into nets.

Inside Submarines

We live inside odd-shaped submarines
chasing after secrets and the darkness of the ocean
on a voyage toward plastic horizons
where vague connections can never be reached
and hopes are not deployed
before the storm arrives and the alarm command starts
to rouse the last illusions to stand up and put life jackets on
looking to each other for help

Once I was at the equator
trying to slice the earth in half along the dotted line
but someone held my hand and said:
"If you do that, friend, water will fall into the void,
and then our submarine
won't have any place to dive."

Phan Nhien Hao

Autumn Song

Like an inverted hat in sunlight and the uselessness of a misplaced article
I realize I don't even resemble myself in old photographs
In newer photographs I am a color reproduction of an outdoor concert without
listeners
Next to kinsmen of a different faith
That was a cloudy day and the faces were retained by flash light
I walked slowly away from the looks

Autumn is like an old immigrant in old clothes
Forlorn and complaining about changes
I am not garrulous, it's just that I can't keep a secret
The hopelessness of unions makes me want to hear
Sounds of leaves falling on a chest
Of a man lying under a tree
With a hand grenade inside his pants pocket

Bread made of buckwheat mixed with some garlic
I don't like tossing food to pigeons in a plaza
They do nothing but peck and copulate
How did aristocrats make love in the past, like pigeons?
Books describe most of them as degenerates
Did they pluck feathers from birds and point at the moon?
If they raped they had to waste a lot of time undressing
People say that my country has been constantly raped!

As a child I spat into the palm of a blind beggar
What should I do now in autumn?

In the Silicon Valley

There are climates that can wear out shoes like acid
The view out the window is always cut by rain and sunlight, and fuzzy
calculations on a computer
I live in a valley where people will saw their own leg to sell to buy a house
All the sublimeness of language has died in a jar breeding an artificial fetus
There are many such artificial children in the Silicon Valley. They wear plastic
name tags and colorful ties

It's not at all difficult to create an impression
Mix arsenic with wine to drink with dragon meat. Look at the sky while stuffing
a hand into your pants pocket to find a morsel of bread without breaking it. Lick
your own sole then stand straight up to greet a crowd attending a funeral. In the
end everything needs to happen exactly according to the daily schedule

Thule is a remote settlement in the Northwest of Greenland only 450 miles from
the top of the world
I want to go there and attempt a journey on dogsled
In this valley even flies can't conceive
Within ten years all the mountains in this place will be upside down triangles
The moon will be pulled to earth by a giant cable
This peninsula will be pushed out to sea by an earthquake then reattached with
super glue

At night a train passes ringing a bell and a barrier is lowered
These are the last sounds of a day in a heaven made of plastic
Before dejection melts with the burning smell of a car collision.

House Without a Door

I live in a house without a door
Each person who visits must bring a door
on his back. Install it before sitting down
then take it with him when he leaves.
My privacy depends on
Visits from these people.

There are those who come empty-handed.
These are extremely poor folks without individuality
Gamblers and punks with pockmarked faces
stop by only to borrow money and swindle.
Spotting them I hastily leave the house
to go visit close friends.

Leaving I also carry a door on my back
(This door I've dislodged from my own house
only to use at other people's houses.)

As the Train Approaches

For me to say this might make a person laugh
infuriate another into plotting a coup d'etat
spoken words really have no weight
like a blue name tag, on a shirt
a 10-year-old student
had gone through two years of calamitous changes.
He often bought iced water during Summer afternoons
hoping to melt the sun
into retangular icebergs.

Growing up I thought speech could heal
open a wound, disinfect, then re-bandage it. I thought…
No, in this silence sometimes I see
memory's two hands reaching out
to clap violently without making a sound
like the wind, like concealed hatred
of souls buried in a mass grave.
This silence exhausts me
it does not forgive, it's like ants,
patiently carrying red corpuscles from my body.

I say this in a screaming voice
But the train lunges forward sounding a horn like thunders
making a mockery of my efforts
On its black side blur these white words:
"Post-Colonial Train, Global Line"
I quickly hop on. Aboard a rabble sit and stand
How many are without tickets like me?

Between the Moon and Seaweed

The man leans a summer ladder
on a moon approaching the eclipse
A car discharges blue smoke
into the daily exhaustion
And biological concerns
gape like fish eyes under ice in the ship's hold
without enough oil to reach the horizon where a rainbow bends down to drink
seawater.

The man and the moon sink down to sleep with seaweed
on a mist-less morning without milk and eggs
without anyone wearing a bronze name tag to open the hotel door ringing a bell
August slowly moves South
on a road redolent of cow manure with three-way intersections
pouncing from abandoned houses
From the picture frame with broken glass there remains
a child's smile.

Night Swim

I swim 150 feet from shore
I'm a good swimmer
The Pacific is 64 million square miles
With that ratio, I'm a microbe in a large basin
To swim beneath stars
simple atoms of the truth
too far away and unable to resolve anything.

The diluted darkness snuffs out all fires
except the glows of jellyfish
I swim until I become
a stranger to my own gravity
and start to sink
at the exact moment the moon is lifted
by a wave-built lever
with my body on this end.

Cutting Hair on the Sidewalk

Cutting hair on the sidewalk
is a means to make money for poor people
and a snobby pleasure for the bourgeoisie

A unique thrill is to have your ears cleaned
a risky bout of comfort
in a historical slumber

Most dangerous is the shaving
a worn out knife expertly sharpened
you must sit still and not have an opinion

Cutting hair on the sidewalk
Remains only in a few countries like Vietnam.

Waiting

On the last day of summer when it was very hot I walked out of the house with a piece of chalk. There was only one street filled with ugly houses uncomfortably facing each other. I walked down the middle wearing a bronze tintinnabulum so that blind men could avoid me. At the end of the street I stopped. There I had an appointment with an airplane with a single wing, a relative I had met only once, and a prophet who could no longer foretell dangerous omens. He was just a grasshopper with its legs broken. While waiting I drew a circle then hopped up and down performing the shaman's rain dance. As usual all those I was waiting for would arrive late. There was only a child passing by. He had the look of an unused but accidentally exposed roll of film. Holding a long rod, he was beating the ground as he walked.

The Old House

This house's falling apart and unnecessarily intricate
even during the day one must fumble along the dark hallways
even a touch can crumble the plaster
glass windows long cracked and unwiped
on the table an ashtray of stagnant water
emanates the smell of cancer.

To this mildewed hallway I've returned
one hand covering my nose the other holding a phone
to talk with professional grave diggers
who'll soon come to plant grass in the garden
time on the ceiling drips on my head
accurately like memory's bullets.

Pho, an Essence

I eat this face
Because it's as tasty as pho, a dish that's made us famous worldwide
I live north of Los Angeles
and must endure a long journey to eat my homeland
From here to Little Saigon is 2 hours by car, to Saigon
is 14 hours by jet. To Hanoi
the furthest point
from me takes more than 30 years.

Eat it, add hot peppers, hoisin sauce, and other impurities. The seasonings
of wandering, of exile.
How to become a professional exile?
Eat it. Look at the hands on the table. They had
probed into the loss of roots
as skillfully as touching a woman's breasts.

I am an exile who craves pho
I don't pretend
And I hate the followers of Derrida, those affecting to resist
an essence.

A Photo from the 60's

Assume this position for a beautiful shot
hand propping up chin, boasting a watch face turned to the front
smile revealing a gold tooth
a blazer borrowed from the studio
(a half portrait,
not showing pants of a different color and plastic flip flops.)

I don't even remember the name of this distant relative
only know that he died soon after
by a bullet
in the 60's.

In the photo his watch showed 10:05,
in what must have been a beautiful day
the young man solemnly sat in front of the camera.
As the light flashed
from the darkness of the camera lens the war could just make out
a young person to lay waste.

Excavations

Wearing a civilizing hat and modern water-proof shoes
I step ashore from a fat ship,
a river-plying ship that does not reach the sea
I am an artist with feathers stuck under the armpits
who flaps his wings walking in the night
beneath the stars to reach a garden
where he digs all night

At sunrise, I have gathered:

The breakages of a child growing up during war, a contempt of ostentatious
games, the enduring loneliness of a wandering exile, a half Western-half
Vietnamese knowledge mixed with cooking oil and sprinkled with black
peppers, the ambition of one who stands in the wing watching the clowns dance
amid foolish applause,

and my own skull,
smeared with dirt and sand.

Sketch for a Self-Portrait

for Loan

This is my life: not beautiful but with some meaning.
This is my mother: also the mother of the sea.
This is my father: a dead man, the rifle next to his body still loaded.
This is my brother: an impotent and loud man.
This is my big sister: half belonging to her husband, half to her underwear.
This is my little sister: squashed by history and money.
This is my wife: my only friend.
This is my daughter: from the darkness of her mother's womb she brought light.
This is my language: half underwater, half on the shore.
This is my people: all hatched from eggs.
This is my country: which counry? I asked.
This is my enemy: identical to me, tired and rail thin.
This is my ancestor: an old stooping monkey,
(Who fed me by shaking the sycamore tree so the figs fell into my mouth)
This is my toy: made of clay.
This is my daily newspaper: all canards,
(The ducks that laid the eggs that hatched into all of us).

This is my life: not for sale.

At The Home of a Fisherman

As the last crow on the power line flew away carrying on its wing a napping bug
I stood alone in a parking lot watching the clouds scrub the sky with fingerless
hands
I hesitated, as usual, by rote, turned the ignition then drove South
Where land bordered sea
Where a fisherman ate seaweed and paved a path with shells leading to a small
house facing the bay
A man who seldom washed but robust like a boiled brown egg
I stayed overnight among fishing rods, rags, and simple tales preserved with salt
redolent of self regard
I woke up twice in the night, once to urinate and once to admire
The stars in the sky
Eyes that do not need a face
I woke up late the fisherman had gone downhill only I remained with sacks of
dried seaweed
And the bay's surface a deep blue
Without a single crow
A perfect day I wanted to acquaint myself with compromises, to eat seaweed,
I wanted to write a couple of simple things, to read a deceased poet
He was also a fisherman
With dreams for baits.

The Sea and Vegetables

I keep the remembrances
returning each night
there's something overly sharp
piercing the top of the head
to die many times in dreams
I sit up
evening is already out there
water spinach drifts all over the ocean
common truths
erode the rocks year round
and I'm only wearing one shoe
to step on the scattered clam shells
the other foot hurting
my left eye sinks deep beneath the white foam
my right eye looks up at the sky
to see the seagulls
dance in the deep blue sky.

Portraits of 3 Overseas Vietnamese (who are not quite patriotic)

I.

Ms. Ly lived more than two decades in Colorado
where there were few Vietnamese and Winter was harsh
she was once a worker in a shoe factory
a packer in a meat plant
a caregiver in a retirement home
now 66 years old she has returned to warm California
she receives 610 dollars in social security a month
this small amount makes everything too expensive for her
when encountering a strange English word on the streets
she writes it down to look up in a dictionary at home
she said: "Only words are free."

Escaping by sea, in the Gulf of Thailand, she had to take it all.

II.

Their hairs are completely white
the wife wears ao dais and the husband out of habit a suit
as when he was a judge in Saigon
they came to the US 15 years ago in the [H.O.] program
all of the husband's strength and youth were buried in the ground
along with manioc roots on the Hoang Lien Son mountains
in 1978 when he was in a reeducation camp
the wife at home twice had to borrow money to buy insecticide
to cook a last meal for herself and their four children
a difficult period, no one had money to lend.

Even now her hand trembles each time she seasons while cooking

III.
This young man is thirty years old
in 1975 he lost his father and an album filled with photos of
happiness
in his own homeland he was branded an enemy
on causes he did not contribute to
this young man came to the US by swimming across the Pacific
for more than a decade he swam during the day and rested on the bottom at
night
arriving, one of his lung has turned into a gill, one into a leaf
of a dead tree
from then on he lived in a glass house
next to jars of insecticide.

In the next life he will come back as a boat.

Summer Migration

All movenents stop
confused around the leaking clock at an intersection
a penguin has been awaken
summer weather, melting ice bergs
crowded flights
I have no place left to migrate

I step along the sidewalk, trying to maintain a distance
between the threatening look of a policeman
and my own anger
I sit in a park to read a newspaper
ink smeared on my hands
on the corner a man stands very straight
an old horn in his hands
reminds me of a roommate
a fan of John Coltrane and somewhat of an alcoholic
now in Chicago
suddenly I remember
a bus ride where I've forgotten an umbrella
a rainy day and the driver with a long scar on the back of his hand
among the different orientations the heterogenous mugs
I have paid a buck to be transported

I read all the classified ads, I finish my submarine
I watch two dogs tussle on the grass
then make a series of brief and high-pitched calls
like the penguins
a beautiful summer day in Santa Monica.

Those Whose Loss Is Only Material

Ashes of a half-burnt cross
and faces pressed into the mud
fingers not tired from playing cards
an answer hidden in small probability
to those whose loss is only material
I say this is a tragic loss caused by spiritual conflicts
because of my principles and your unprincipled enthusiasm
on the field in the evening too many fell to be reaped by the Angel of Death
they could no longer live to evade taxes
to finish out a war
I say this lost is not just material
this is a tragic loss caused by spiritual conflicts
we have made the dawns bleed.

To X. and I

If I am an immoral sadness
then you are the old direction
protecting the night flights
I walk on bridges connecting two alien shores
my hand holding on to nagging curses
then you are a small dictionary
defining secret words to me

The brief long-distant phone conversation
interrupted by a civil war and coup d'etats
midway there's a broken bench
where I sit clutching flowers
then you are a tourist photographing
me among courteous people
arriving from afar.

NGUYEN HUU HONG MINH was born in 1971 in Da Nang, and now lives in Ho Chi Minh City. A journalist by trade, he is the author of *A Vague Voice*, poetry (1999), *Drain the Bottom*, stories (2000), *Sustaining Substance and other poems*, poetry (2002), *Word Fringe*, poetry (2003), *A Stranger at Midnight*, stories (2004) and *A Historical Black Hole*, poetry (2004). He is best known for the poem, "A Historical Black Hole," published on Tiến Vệ in 2003. In 2005, he was invited to Munich, Germany, where he gave a reading with To Thuy Yen.

A Historical Black Hole

Often he sees his male member in Saigon,
His head in Hanoi
His arms and legs abandoned somewhere in Soc Trang
Morning in the Central, afternoon in the South,
Evening in the North, night in the West
A glass of coffee looking out at the Turtle Tower bitter as his blood
A bout of madness at Ma Toc temple, days and months spent in Kenh Xang
Cambodian women, O the figures and complexion burdened with so much
worries!
Wisps of smoke like nooses enticing him to hang himself
Often in dreams he sees himself already dead. A rotten corpse, picked by crows.
He's delighted by that!

His soul hung from some pubic hair of a Hai Phong girl whoring in China
Babbling in Vinh Long, kissing ass in Can Tho, legs spread wide in Ca Mau,
Shaving in Bac Lieu, madly contorted in Ha Khau, horny in Sa Pa, drunk in Lao
Cai
Mouth still shouting Dang Thieu Quang, die Quang!*
Cursing in Hue, making a ceremonial offering in Quang Binh, holding his prick
pissing in My Son and shitting in Hoi An
Fucking on the Thu River and eating pussy on the Perfume River
Hacking and spitting on the Gianh River, a chase and a knife fight on the Han
River
Contemptuous of the Viet race on the Red River, disparaging the Chinese race
on the Nam Thi River

He cut out each slice of life to hide in his creative work
Callow thoughts have grown hair inside his skull box as hard as a rock
His essence is Communism, Communism!
He laughs crookedly like a historical black hole
In panic and fear he realizes he's still alive though working with corpses
Zigzagging like a ghost, possessed by the devil's soul who's always tricking him
into committing foolish and bizarre acts
He wants to make love to Nguyen Thi Thu Hue**—He's ruthless about that
He wants to rape Le Thi My Y—He hankers after that
He cannot be aroused by Phan Thi Vang Anh—He's certain about that
He loves Ly Hoang Ly—He will always hold that sacred
He's fearful of Vi Thuy Linh's crack—He's terrified of that
Mankind crawl from the crotch—He asserts that fact
The Vietnamese race is vagina-crazy—He confirms that

Nguyen Huu Hong Minh   183

But when he needs his male member it's forgotten in Saigon
When he needs his head it's discarded in Hanoi
When he needs to flap his arms and legs they're abandoned in Ca Mau
In a dream he's confused about what he has said to Bac Lieu, Soc Trang, An Giang***
Spread legs! Let's spread legs!
He shouts with the sounds of the asshole...

Saigon 12/2003

Translator's notes:
*Dang Thieu Quang is a poet, novelist and friend of Nguyen Huu Hong Minh
**Nguyen Thi Thu Hue, Le Thi My Y, Phan Thi Vang Anh, Ly Hoang Ly and Vi Thuy Linh are contemporary female writers.
*** Bac Lieu, Soc Trang and An Giang are cities in the Mekong Delta

PHAN HUYEN THU was born in Hanoi in 1972 and still lives there. She comes from a musical family, her father a celebrated song composer, her mother a famous singer. Phan Huyen Thu herself has performed publicly on various traditional instruments. A journalist and screen-writer by profession, she is a playwright and author of two collection of poems, *Lying on my Side* (2001) and *Empy Chest* (2005), and a book of stories, *Wooden Gecko* (2003). Her works have also been translated into English and published in *The Literary Review* and "Of Vietnam: Identities in Dialogue" (Palgrave 2001). In an interview, she said: "Sometimes I feel like I'm writing for someone else. I don't join, don't get unruly, I write quietly and softly, like breathing. I write hesitantly, falteringly, I write then erase, then write calmly and coldly. Done, I feel emptied out and vaguely nostalgic."

Begging

My hand can't reach the year 2,000
can't touch the nearest man.

My hand
latches on to stray clouds
waiting for a rain drop.

My hand
is used up and redundant
now attached to the bed board
now worn out and sucked

Do you know, brother,
I still stick my hand out

Maybe in the next century
there'll be a day

Phan Huyen Thu

Hue

Night slithers slowly into the Perfume River
an elongated note breaks under Trang Tien bridge

A Nam Ai dirge of widowed concubines*
fishing for their own corpse from a boat on the river

To be king for a night in the imperial capital
go now, make a poem for purple Hue

Shattering symmetry voluntarily
with a tilted conical hat
        an askew carrying pole
                eyes looking askance
Hue is like a mute fairy
crying inside without speaking.

I want to murmur to Hue and to caress it
but I'm afraid to touch the sensitive spot on Vietnam's body.

1997

Translator's note:
*lines 3, 4, and 5 allude to the prostitutes plying their trade on sampans on the
Perfume River. They are "widowed" because their kings, the johns, leave them
after one night.

Moving Along The Edge Of Summer

Moving along the edge of summer
An early moon bends the first third of the month
Gaudily fawning
vain wild flowers trail the rails of a provincial station
On the roof of a forgotten train car
The odor of sunlight sleeps deeply

Because of an immortal and tuneful ideal
a lovelorn cricket trips over a dew drop
A lizard warrior clucks its tongue and drinks up the night
dreams a thin dream of mosquito wings
Stringing up faith a female spider
clasps a sack of saturated eggs

Having drank a dream by mistake
My wooden gecko sobbed all last night
Leading itself along the edge of summer
Finding a way to fall.

4/10/1999

Sad Song

On dry land with light flesh
the body wants to fly into the glowing yellow
wind
achingly blue arc

To swallow mutterings
to suppress weakness
to smirk

You're there
right here
a thousand soundless
shouts away

I go out,
buy yellow chrysanthemums
to place by window
autumn wilting

Chest cracked into a buzzing bee hive
zipping in a hundred directions
to sting the night swollen
sad written characters

10/4/02

190

The Eighth Month

Women like to make their own
seasons. For no reason
my blood pressure drops. For no reason
my heart skips a beat. Suddenly
I'm cold
all over. A low pressure expanse
wants to start a revolution. Wants
to overturn the female virtues. Wants
to grab another's spouse. Wants
to blow up the monument. Wants
to join the decadent crowd. Wants
to take part in the cultured journey. Wants
to chirp on about self during a meeting. Wants
the hedge to tip over the dodder to climb. Wants
water to be higher than boat. Wants
storm number 3 to pass over Hainan Island. Wants
storm number 4 to not land on Hong Kong. Wants
to be drunk in the rain. Wants to love
a solitary person. Wants
own jaw to be locked. Wants
to be unconscious. Wants
to be under a spell. Wants
to be oblivious.

But the eighth month. Autumn
laughs weakly. Its sounds snigger high above.

8/1/03

Chest Empty

I sigh
winter chill chest empty
sadness far away affection also far away

Fleeing flesh to spurt towards ceiling
looking down at curled up corpse
bawling at bed corner

Out on the boulevard
trash trucks rumble
a pyre of nylon trash bags
two lovers burnt crisp
an injured vet heavy chested with medals
still shouts one two marches on without rest
she jilted
luffa flower cuddles cotton shirt
lullabies
Thoai Khanh—Chau Tuan*
boiling sniveling guts the avocado.

Alley
sharply drawn round moon drifting
girls without husbands tormented by drugs
sob
my hair with yellow and silver
brown purple and blue strands
moonlight lies soggy in measured sorrow

under western eaves kids
far from innocence
with heads on books of astrology hugging each other
sleeping deeply through cat screams
realism
be romantic!
one two three
let's fly up high.

Chest empty.

Translator's note:
*actors of *cai luong* folk opera, which is usually mournful with much weeping.

The Remains of the Evening

Sadness interminable dusk. Sadness
pours from ten dazed fingertips. Sadness
is blood. Spreading out waiting for the moon to rise
so as to glitter. Clotting on flesh. (As if having
an internal wound. But I myself
am the evening's wound.)

Sadness is space. I sawed myself against the blue sky
of my own mocking eyes. Sadness
pours from my hair. Each strand dripping blood. Chest heavy
from the pressure of a betrayal. Unable to breathe
I close my eyes. Trying to hear
each drop of blood crawl patiently from my hair
to soak into the earth. Sprouting
love's end.

A passionate flower cannot bloom
under the light of banality. A seed
drifts with the jealous wind. Dropping
on the treacherous ground. Magnanimity's discounted. The garden plot
strains to be attentive. Forcing me
to gestate revenge anxiously. But
sadness has emptied itself out. I don't have another
drop of blood left. On my head. My hair
also drifts with the red rays
of sunset.

Pretending to yank the horizon. A glimpse
from you. Hiding from the wind's smile. You look
at my feet where the sad worms
are wriggling and crawling up my knees. Arranging
a new pattern of despair. You run
from my sadness in the evening
to lunge headfirst into the night surely. The roots
wisely decline the gentle deception. Wilted love
inside a vase containing a mixture of petty things.

Phan Huyen Thu

I've bled all of my sad blood
on an evening standing on tiptoe. Proud.
When night comes. I've only two leg tubes left
and a few self-deluded worms. Wriggling. And
tucked into the crack of my big toe. And. A voice
or something like that... as
your icy look.

4/20/05

VAN CAM HAI was born in 1972 in Hue, where he still lives. A writer for Hue television, he is the author of the collection *Man Who Tends The Waves* (1995), and two travel books, covering Europe and Tibet, respectively. His poems have been translated into English and published in *The Literary Review, Tinfish, Of Vietnam: Identities in Dialogue* (Palgrave 2001) and *Three Vietnamese Poets* (Tinfish 2001).

Remembering the Time When Men Appeared as Ghosts

On the edge of the Pacific we rub against each other
the sandy hills are like thousands of buttocks awakened to dance
the tide rising and ebbing are stupefying a billion bodies
death is lighting a wedding candle
to walk again behind the shadows of children
and it calls to the ghosts
resuscitating a life cycle blooming every twenty centuries
sit right here and be calm in this dark house your armpits
body hairs are chasing the breast species
the lit realm
is running pell mell crisscrossing all the beds
the white blanket, the yellow blanket, the black and the red blankets
cannot cover this thirst
the fantasies of tongues
You and I fumbling to clean up this final mess.

Van Cam Hai

Spatial Recognition

The clouds are menstruating in the sky far from
the blue arch of the underpants
yet the feet of the mountains and the rivers lurk
in the evening when bullets become drops of blood
falling and illuminating your home
raindrops tumbling down your rib like a spiraling groove
        sucking in the gun barrel
suddenly as I was walking through the village
my enthusiasm asphyxiated by Mother's bamboo basket
an embryo crawled out bawling peace
the clouds are busy laundrying the storm
inside the bathtub the earth is still menstruating
a bullet sits waiting
to fall on whose home

The Rivers Have Not Only Me

Vietnamese rivers are often contemplative
cloud levels of memories
slurp the sad grass a mouthful of blue river
on the body convulsed with laughter bomb craters reflect back at the sun
from high above a tongue wanders
her language is a tireless light spread evenly, in spite of the sleepwalking rain,
the roof of a church, a pier, a dry log like death leaning against your porch
my pain does not have a flowering or fruit-bearing season
night barks at a face with countless pimples
a rose holds a gun
my heart
a flame-blowing tube
a time when words fall asleep drunk next to the wood-burning stove
a hand spits out a well-chewed death expression
my brother's previous life
a blind tv
still I watch till the end of the card game
a cigarette burns a naked body
a car collapses on its knees having won the eternity prize
even if someone does howl a dirge tomorrow
O my scent don't you borrow from a deficit
To the rivers is added a little sister's waist
filled with the self-confidence to seduce the map of the world.

Death and Sister

Evenings where the dew bulges breasts
a fervent lulling prayer from a silent mouth
has strangled my sister
while she was repenting
life is conceived from death
tears swim and dive like honeysucking bees
punctured
a statue of christ shatters and returns to the earthly void
to let my sister bend over and carry a smile piggyback
to a serene place.

January 20th

A string plucked
hastily carries a love duet
I become my shadow's shadow
a dreamt night does not drink sweetly from a cup of wine
because the thousand-year-old figure has been parted
to guard time with a broken vigil
the one-hundred-and-first egg, the married couple forget to hatch a new legend
continuing to step from a chest, the Daily Tear River pokes its body into the sea
countless mosquitoes cling white to the shore of the eye, they crystallize in the
deeps
a sky without needs for a hat
a sky without needs for an appendix
a sky bluer than your spinal column in touch with two realms
a heart with a mythical length
a labor strike
a selling of one's body without interest
a civilization
premonitions

Flower Temple

unripe description
untamed news
a meteoric word destroys the ozone layer
a thin petal blossoms a parachute a flare
spring wears a warm scarf
tolerance
on the river a sprawled derrick transforms
summer white bamboo shoot thighs
curfew
the handkerchief drips a mulberry finger
is someone a piggy bank for you to break the saved days
autumn exposes the sun drenched itinerary
step on a shadow advertising a memory item
the humid sounds of cicadas the earlobe acts up
winter
fragrant rice crispies a late transition
scrawny blue
life already ruined you continue to live famously outside sympathies
because of hypersensitivity the earth is daily discounted
unlike you a reciprocal memory
a sole slow dying fate of man

Deluge

Rain strangles the veranda
you are infected white the flow of night is level
I harried
shrunken the kitchen
a browbeating chest fries the air
a few steps though not colorful, you sidle through the door: 5 limes/5 fire
fingers
a rain alley slow to answer
the head of the storm surges forward searching for a prey
an urban nest
street intersections spill out on strike
the poet stretches
wears each phrase of loose fitting narrative
from the peak saliva and blood are jealous of each other
the calm hem of your dress the neighbors climb up to rebuild a leaky fantasy
paralyzed
you do not look at the sky through a rare crack my wound
the street looks askance and knits
a scarf turns out the light
the prying day leaves this life
clueless
a laughing round

Academic Garden

Colliding with libraries
the fort of Athens is stranded on a draft manuscript
the vast academic garden a copy Judas's tongue bends a computer finger
against philosophy pain intermingles with man
S.O.S. about me
poetry tastes artillery
a bowl of poison reminds the rooster to crow loudly
strums the mourning cloth
the waste land dreams
peasants overflows vegetation
leisurely drive breakfast to assist the dawn
village philosophy
does not copy anyone's harvest season

A Morning Purposely Lazy

My house forgets to scrub the midday hours
rain sometimes sews prayers through the mosquito netting
a dim hole
chases tinkling
you still wear an illusion you a person lining a dream
take it all off to go on the lush streets the palm of a hand
a self-pitying foetus
grass rushes into the night cage
a switch chews making hissing sounds
punctuation dissolves my life
rock toss sing and play music
the furniture emits sex voluntarily
the entire wedding the giraffe sings you a scorching song a propositioning
phone call
pours down a rock cliff a trill of blue veins
a nuclear bomb moves a conference
I don't hear a hawk seduces power
I hear myself in the morning fragrant a ladle of water
a prehistoric man limps and hums to prevent a drought
your heart is still a sidewalk for me to stroll

Eternal

Alien with night
the eye of the poinciana dances
slimy
hairy tail of a cow swinging praying for a bright star
sweeping the street noisily the primordial smell aches
crime jungle
wild deer lunge a blue streak
idol
beautiful a corpse encrusted with sand from the next life
intelligent her face obscure a rice paddy made of glass
a long musical instrument hills and mountains pressing confused notes
yours and my family sing at will, each melody making us feel as whole as a rice
grain
in front of a house of odd geometry
Plato ogling a cathedral to mother's milk
at that moment a giant dust cloud
the black bronze face of suicide
the outer ear hovering the neuron knot eager at the root of a hair
a big city spittle flooding an artery
overflowing a blood pocket embarking on a train to all directions
smuggling a poem burying a ghost fallen on its side inside the seventh sense
love market
still new
only me tottering
a hierarchical smile
the carriage driver
ambling a horse kicks

PHAN BA THO was born in Da Nang in 1972, and now lives in Ho Chi Minh City. "A faded, empty organism," he once described himself. After being unemployed for 60 months, 8 days and 4 hours, he's now working as a lawyer. The author of the samizdats, *Vertical Movement* (2001) and *Endless Trash Pile*, his poems appear regularly in many print and web journals.

craving everything & they... ate what to live [and shout]

poet tran dan sat leaning against the dark shadow of a wall for half a century: he craved light & ate **the town's gate** [1]

poet dang dinh hung, born in an era of food shortage he **wanted to eat an entire market**

poet [wide mouthed, of the crass young generation / of **candied fruits and strange pier**] nguyen huu hong minh: **ate a seaport**

tran tien dung ate an entire **chicken feather duck feather sky**

linh dinh ate: **the most beautiful word**[s]. le dat a word porter, ate: **word shadows**. especially shadows of words... abutting [toilets / stairs / overpasses / fortune]

nguyen quoc chanh ate: **the identity papers [of metaphors]** and **inanimate weather**
bui chat **ate scraps of paper, corpses** & even **pussies left over** [... in a seminary]

vi thuy linh ate salty food [causing her to always scream in public: i'm **thirsty**] thirsty, o mom i'm thirsty

basically they craved from the most ordinary to the most bizarre and ghastly [valid] & ate and drank insolently, vehemently everything

there are those who **beg from the past** [amateurishly] & a bunch who **beg from literature** [fateful]

nguyen huy thiep ate: [**daffodil**] **flowers** & chattered with shit [a rumor: all vietnamese
writers in or out of the country are not only lukewarm and ignorant, worthless. but are shit, shit, all of them shit]

tran dang khoa [fastidious – in poetry and painting] only ate pretty thin stuff [... **falling slantwise**]. for example: extra thin with wings**. or with 2 extra thin wings. ate it all

although, if compared to the old and seasoned [in cash & confusion] then all of them are just a bunch of cute children or at most seeds for the future in a country [betraying poetry & full of prostitutes]

it is said, poets with a foot in the ministry of politics are fierce, truly tough. they
are champions of fasting. are true hunger artists & high-class acrobats.
O, O... [of course] they eat nothing. yes, truly

yes, they chew nothing [beside the people & the nation]

saigon 11/30/2004

Translator's notes:
*words in bold indicate names of poems or collections of poems of poets
mentioned and not mentioned
**phrase taken from a tampon advertisement

Nude Self Portrait

to thuy hang & kim hoa

if only I could slip into the ground [or] run disappearing
into something, it'd be fantastic
yesterday I was stripped naked in the middle of a highway, 80,000 people
like metaphors and are unclear about motives
pity only to the small children who were present
very difficult, lecturing on how to mix a cocktail
with a handful of crooked bones / wrinkled lines
convoluted and sad + plus
the natural rudeness of the curious mob
people inspected my body / up down and sideways randomly
they saw in my armpit... yes, nothing but a forest with trees
straight, chopped down, completely burnt
with two eyes yellowed by beer froth & unbelievably horny, yesterday
I – was – stripped – naked – on – a – mat – torn
ragged & reeking a foul smell
(too many people glorify this filth)
they touched my hair / cheek nose & beckoned others
I saw a group of american soldiers, toying with their mouths
saddam's hair gleefully
I became jealous of him / I thought, he's truly happy
those in white coats liked to confirm the dna / because they've heard
to be that mad, one must eat horses' balls
what could they read on my body
they could become wiser than that, a little... yes, if
they'd pry my mouth open
they'd probably see a prick I've been sucking for a long time, big and tall, inside
Wei Hui said: this object can spin 360 degrees & should be used
once and thrown away
but I prefer Mian Mian*
[both sort of crazy and sane]
but, very importantly / the marvelous quality in her:
fuck first, pay later / love – being in debt, also decent

Translator's note:
*Wei Hui and Mian Mian are contemporary Chinese writers.

MIEN DANG was born in Da Nang in 1974, came to the US in 1989, and now lives in Florida, where she works as a manicurist. She has been partially deaf since the age of 13. Mien Dang has studied meditation with the Burmese monk Sayadaw U Silananda and the Vietnamese monk Sayadaw U Khippa. Her poems can be seen regularly in various Vietnamese print and web journals. English translations of her work have appeared in the webzines *xconnect* and *MiPoesias*.

Portrait

I know the bud will bloom
Perhaps into a girlish pink
Or the color of a salamander
Or the color of a hairy worm
Grinding a thousand leaves
To steal for itself a green color

How does one know that someone is longing to look at a green flower?!

Perhaps the blossom will not be whole
Missing a broken angel wing
The flower also has no perfume
But I'm longing for something else entirely

And he doesn't have a penis
Twisting towards me on a VERY HUMAN foot
And I also don't have a vagina
We make love with our mouths
With tongues sucking
To increase our pleasures
We clang our teeth
God has given mankind so many marvelous sensations!
If there really is an actual nervous system
We'd knock each other down to make love
Damn those illusions!

I know the bud will bloom into a mottled flower
With fake angel wings
But I solemnly wait for something else entirely

And he doesn't have a penis
Circling me on a VERY HUMAN foot

Dec 5, 2001

Laugh!

Abandon yourself
The window bar decanters the slanting sunlight
Shape of a creature that knows how to sulk
Urgent howls of crazy love talks
Curse in the filthiest language
Let's try to kiss each other
I borrow the soft parts of the lips
To reconstruct a ravaged face
Rotating upward the pupils
Roots like tangled lightning elongate
Reddened the cruel dawn
Doddering love's black magic
Killer pupils
Doubts then modesty
On pale pink cheeks
The skin has become musty here
In panic the river licks the bank
Joy erupts
And who are you?
I save for you grief on round breasts
How can I wait?
And what would I be?
What's repulsive hidden deep inside the uterus
I want to pierce shame into you
And what would we be?
I want to see you laugh
A trembling puppet bursting
A hand on shrunken testicles
Opening wide the flat chest
Flash frozen the self-absorbed lonely substance
To escape raggedness by stripping naked
Tickle and laugh
Laugh!

Jan 26, 2002

Naked

Him nude
Beauty flays along the length of the dirty stain
Petrified in some corner nibbling
Phosphorescent glass shards
Sweet tasting half a curse
The remaining secret part
Groaning behind clenched teeth

Him nude
Slippery inside a body oozing water
Night is pinned with a million black sesame seeds
Flitting along the fireflies
He is buried alive at the fold
I nudge it out gingerly
The green scar by chance passes through many springs

Him nude
Skin brownish yellow the color of alluvium
Pores sprouting
The life force splits the mud cakes
Naked to be reborn

Can't Speak Yet

Extending the color of sunshine,
He touches the blue shadow of the sky.
The sharp tip of pregnancy
Seduces
A flipped jaw.
Existence drifts completely the soul,
Frothing an ape dream.
Carousing.
The subconscious warps the other side of the face.
Cruelty crowds passion into a corner,
Rams the body as the flame rises.
A short nerve
Softens the water.
Calamity ridicules:
Let's pierce to pieces the illusion!
Appearance bares its back whispering.
The hand not black enough for the heart of night.
Cannot speak now.
Striving for meaning at the end,
In a cattle state,
Stretched out the wet eye...

Sept 12, 2002

Seasoned

The abyss blooms tenderly in the crotch,
flips the body.
The hallucination casts a strange face the submerged pains.
I listen to a music bored into bones and marrows.
If it's that absurd,
then be quiet in front of too many masks to morph into.

Primordial,
       a red skinned sack kicking madly,
and still the scalding drop life's endless night.
Heed the arousal both deranged and sensibly elastic:
a secret pliant stain,
the shape of a worm slipping smoothly into earth.
Vibrate the end-of-the-world thread.
Recall   a   torn   feeling.
Nods repeatedly that head,
gaze at that grinning darkness,
and memorize a poem about that little mouse.
All is intimate and forgiving,
challenging the dark
               and chaos.
Blood clears a course drifts down a blind dream,
boils the pit of a girl's soul.

From this strange hairy bush, an endless question.
From you to me, walking into an alliance
                      of life
                      and death.

If you want to kill yourself, then try to forget all blunders.
I'll give up my self-torture
so you could be reborn as downy hair over my ears.
Fondling each vague photographic negative,
life gushes out,
beats urgently on your river banks.
Morning in the highland juts out like tiny cheeks,
clear and plump,
applauds the enthralled heart and mind.
All things on earth need to be seen, sucked and sniffed,
carefully and attentively, by the earthiest organs:
the nose of a wild dog, a milk-fed mouth, eyes of a rainy evening.

A monologue.
Look into the pit of a toilet,
sniff for your lover's sweat,
and suck your own tongue.
Live,
        experience a surprise attack and resist without tiring.
Memory of spirited life will sweep clean messy remembrances—
find the pulsing artery of the frenzy.
It appears the man is crying,
              set aside the smell of a forest silently burning,
shattering sounds of a newly formed desert.
The animal instinct of spitting out whole the poison,
suddenly sadly naked...
Never tasted to the full the saltiness of salt,
a bout of sea rain on the tip of the tongue.
A rousing root spreads across the lips,
                  to life's climax.
No   need   for   another   escape.
Stroke aslant the worries
        from my breast
            with your hand.

Feb 17, 2005

Losing Your Pants

It's dismal to be naked,
but let's peel this earth into fragments.
Examine from the rude red infants to those who've lost their pants.
All dismal.

Out of recklessness,
space is always stabbed or torn,
fast and strong,
to discover intoxications.
Let's sympathize with raggedness,
as in losing your pants,
as in being very naked…

Pity those who grasp things by mistake,
they are thieves who are quite lovely.
One day the thief suddenly loses his pants.
Do you know, friend,
since he doesn't have pants he pisses interminably,
the liquid escaping to the sea.

The truth is made worse by anger,
those are the most wretched moments in life.
You can stuff paper into the gaps to keep warm.
You can speak nonstop to escape loneliness,
dry the little ants just rescued from swirling water,
hear till the end the trembling of soggy dragonfly wings.
Then peel all of yourself—
so no pants remain to be lost.

Smiling stupidly,
feel a soft dumb loving tongue…
To swallow whole a man in poetry
is to knock down a tumultuous world hounding one's mind.
Concentrating hard to hear a two-way conversation,
to solve the secret of losing your pants.

Mien Dang

Losing your pants
Losing your pants
Losing your pants

It's dismal to be naked.

July 29, 2006

Old Female Poet

The moon shines unexpectedly on her chest,
the young woman opens her eyes wide to look at her hands.
She has come to this life to leave behind a small moan,
leave behind spiteful hatred,
leave behind soft dust clinging to her hair,
leave behind distinctions,
leave behind a body cut by grass,
leave behind selfish jealously,
leave behind everything
to grow old.

An old lady passes by leaving behind a young heart.
Her poetry is impassive at the dining room table,
listening in silence to the clamors of chopsticks and bowl
in place of loving words.

July 29, 2006

AI VAN QUOC was born in 1975 near Thai Binh, studied at the National University in Hanoi, and is now working in Japan. He has published widely in Vietnamese print and web journals in and outside of Vietnam, and has also translated several Japanese and Chinese poets into Vietnamese, including Shuntaro Tanikawa and Ye Hui.

Echo from a Puddle

misty morning one autumn day
awake
a mayfly
sunning itself
dead
on the pa-so-kon keyboard
(abbreviation of "personal computer," according to those from the land of the
rising sun)

mayfly
from where
drifting here
sunning itself
then dies, without knowing it

one mayfly
only
one mayfly dead
but so much
musing

one misty morning
remembering

by the window
of parent's house
let muck worms wiggling in a puddle
eat
sesame salt

by the window
of dormitory
let muck worms like those
eat
sesame salt

Ai Van Quoc

let muck worms like those
eat
sesame salt
by the puddle
in land of the rising sun

childhood day
had a flash: invite them to eat what I like to eat
(nothing fancy, but at one time, sesame/peanuts were not available even, "white
rice with sesame salt" had become something like a "specialty")

in school yard
fleetingly understood:
precisely
those muck worm friends
from that distant puddle

in land of the rising sun
who's calling
from a night puddle
"O friend, I've come"

muck worms anywhere
in this world's puddle
are still muck worms

no doubt
each of us is
a muck worm
in universe's puddle
(thought derived from Buddha: dog, bug, worm, fly, all have Buddha nature)

poetry/letters written
by
muck worms
delivered from puddle
speaking a human language
and
arranging words with pa-so-kon

there are other muck worms
speaking a human language
and never knowing pa-so-kon
(desiring to be human strolling, telling stories: not only in the mountainous
regions of Mu Cang Chai, or fishing village by Cambodia's Tonle Sap, but, even
in places like London or Tokyo there are illiterates)

everything: with human hands, muck worms can write poems
plant trees
plow fields
work machines
(folk poetry has an author: "our hands can make everything, with human power
even rocks and pebbles can become rice")
and
even
holy war—like Bush, father and son, and Osama bin Laden

from a night autumn puddle
echoes:
if you, like Osama, know how to let others, like Bush, eat sesame salt, or,
conversely,
more practically,
if you, like those bosses, all know
how to watch muck worms in world's puddle
(voice of muck worm in puddle, inside Hanoi's royal citadel,* or anywhere else)

Tokyo, 9-2006

*The wells and gutters inside Hanoi's royal citadel—discovered by chance (having been lusted after for years by researchers specializing in Hanoi, often known as "Hanoi scholars")—are being carefully dug up and preserved, similar to other discoveries (of wells and gutters) the world over, from ancient Greek civilization, for example, or from the Tang and Sung Dinasties. Next to golden trays, bowls of precious gems, knife blades and ceramic shards, archeologists have also discovered living creatures, ossified from hundreds or thousands of years ago, such as crickets, even muck worms, bugs or larvas.

In late autumn of last year, accompanied by an elderly friend who's obsessed with archeology in Japan, I visited an old tomb just excavated. People were buzzing: the tomb belonged to the queen of Ito—a small country encountered by a Chinese envoy going from the Korean peninsula to the capital of a very short race, the Nu (ancestors to today's Japanese; this journey was recorded as "Tale of the Nu People" in the "Wei Chih" chronicles, written in the 3rd century A.D.; there are those who doubt the authenticity of these accounts.) The news spread quickly through the town. Beside himself, my friend phoned nonstop, and even drove over to pick me up. Arriving, we were shocked. It turned out to be just a gutter! Only one! A horde of newspaper reporters. Even more numerous, those obsessed with archeology. (a.v.q.)

A Crack on the Wall

> *Night dreaming, saw a crack on the temple wall*
> *Day dreaming, lazed on a mossy shrine floor*
> *(a.v.q.)*

Madness and Enlightenment arrived when
perhaps when man blossomed from a frog eye*

Madness and Enlightenment
a crack
on a Tibetan temple's wall
reappear
on Tay Ninh's high tower
spread
scent of mother Nara's house**

Madness and Enlightenment
have been living among
a black sun
red air

Madness and Enlightenment
rising from the sea
became
AM, EM***
clearly AM was Madness and EM Enlightenment
(back then the sun was black and the air red)

Madness and Enlightenment
emerging from a cave
grass boat
lily pad steps
(legend goes: just before that era, the sun turned red, the air turned desolate, so,
the human eyes being color-blind, confused black with red, red with black)

Ai Van Quoc

Enlightenment
hiding
in Royal Palace
emitted smoke
ignored man
(because: back then man was in chaos, only knew Madness, no longer knew
Enlightenment)

now and then
Enlightenment
appears
as tidal wave
as its children run to the sea, yelling "Bô"****
(I don't understand, why my people are not told to run to the forest to yell "Ma."
Although they still know that Ma is Mother Matter returning from the green-
robed Goddess of the Forest, and the white-robed Goddess of the River)
unruly children
the sea storm raged on

Madness and Enlightenment
are both brother and sister
both husband and wife
(in the beginning: around the hill one time, brother and sister became wife and
husband)
both male and female

Madness and Enlightenment
are both a gentleman and a nobody
a lady and a whore
(reflecting: one day stuck in a whorehouse, the next day wielding a magistrate's
whip)*****
both day and night

Madness and Enlightenment
neither sister nor brother
neither wife nor husband
(only after becoming wife and husband did they recognize each other, so
from that point on, not knowing whether to be wife and husband or sister and

brother, they had turn into lime, so as to become a rock of a woman holding a
child, waiting for her husband)
neither female nor male

MADNESS and ENLIGHTENMENT
neither nobody nor gentleman
neither whore nor lady
neither night nor day

MADNESS and ENLIGHTENMENT
are two yet one
are one yet two

Madness and Enlightenment
both existing and not
not "is"/not "Madness"
not "not"/not "Enlightenment
(a Japanese monk: Mahayana scriptures don't suppose that "is" is "Madness,"
and "not" as "Enlightenment")

frog eye brazen
one frog eye
gives birth to
two human eyes

but man has forgotten: all derived from a frog eye
MADNESS = ENLIGHTENMENT
ENLIGHTENMENT = MADNESS

ENLIGHTENMENT is simply
a crack
on the wall
like
MADNESS

man's secret
cracks
on the wall

Eastern Japan, 9-2006

----

*"frog eye": let's go and admire the Tibetan temples, look at the results of explorations by Westerners and Japanese.
**"mother Nara": the foundation of the pantheist religion Tenrikyo, based in Western Japan.
***"AM and EM": ADAM and A, EVA and UM, that is ADAM/EVA (Christianity) and A/UM (Lamaism).
****"Bố": Father Dragon, Lạc Long Quân, the mythical father of the Vietnamese race
*****A reference to Nguyen Du's "Truyện Kiều," where the protagonist was transformed from a whore to a magistrate (a.v.q.)

HOANG DA THI was born in 1978 in Hue, and now lives in Ho Chi Minh City. She is the author of the collection *Breast Bells* (1988), comprised of poems spoken by her when she was between 3 and 5, and recorded by her mother, poet Lam Thi My Da. The father also appeared as Mr. Wall. (No wallflower or whimsical invention, "Wall" was his first name.) English translations of her poems have appeared in *xconnect*.

There Is A Person

There is a person riding his bike on the street
He has an entire mole under his mouth
That is Mr. Wall

There is a person who is all black and smudgy
And stands all night next to the stove
That is the kitchen door

There is a person whose nerves ache
Who writhes silently without anyone knowing
That is a guitar

Hoang Da Thi

A Black Mole

A person's life lies inside a slipper
Mr. Wall walks by
His black mole falls in
He walks home
Touches his face to find the black mole gone
He runs to the slipper
But does not see the black mole
He runs out to the yard immediately
Pinches some dirt into a black mole
Then attaches it to his face
People who come by to visit
All say:
Mr. Wall has a mole made of dirt

An Elephant and Uncle Vy

Uncle Vy has an elephant eye and an Uncle Vy eye
At the zoo
An elephant has an Uncle Vy eye and an elephant eye
Uncle Vy swaps mouths with the elephant
Uncle Vy's mouth has a trunk he eats sugarcane
When he walks on the street whoever sees him says
Hey, hey, a man who eats with an elephant's mouth
While at the zoo
There is an elephant who eats with Uncle Vy's mouth
That's why he eats rice all day

Hoang Da Thi

Snoring

Lim is sleepy
She writes a snoring poem
She does a great job
All the lines are the same
She asks mother for a piece of paper
She writes on both sides
Then she nails the piece of paper to a wall
On the four corners are four nails
She names the poem: Snoring
Whoever comes to Lim's house
Has to read Lim's poem
People read: zzz, zzz, zzz...

Breast Bells

Mother's two breasts are two bells
I touch them
They go: Kreng, kreng, kreng....
I borrow the breast bells
I go sell ice cream
Whoever hears the breast bell sounds has to buy
Breast ice cream is very sweet
Kreng, kreng, kreng....

Mr. Wall Borrows A Shadow

Mr. Wall does not have a shadow
He borrows a shadow from Mr. Yes
He walks on the street
Everyone who meets him says
Mr. Wall does not have a shadow
Mr. Wall does not have a shadow

A Plastic Mask

A plastic mask
Knows how to cry
Knows how to be sad
Knows a pineapple
Knows an umbrella
Knows a bucket
Knows a mosquito netting
Knows a spider
Knows the moon
Knows a pair of shoes
Knows a flower
Knows a grain of rice
Knows a plastic face

Hoang Da Thi

Star Buttons

The sky is like a roof
The sky is like a shirt
A shirt has many buttons
Those are star buttons

People Make Cakes

The moon
Sleeps all day
Runs around all night
He runs and falls down
To this earth
In the morning
People take it home to make cakes

This Mother Has

This mother has
A very tasty breast
O breast o breast
Let me reach you
A fresh grass breast
A horizon breast

LY DOI was born in 1978 in Quang Nam and now lives in Ho Chi Minh City. A member of the Open Mouth group, he has been published widely on webzines and in group samizdats such as *Six-Sded Circle* (2002) and *Open Mouth* (2002), and in his own samizdats, *Seven Spider Improvisations* and *Dogmeat Vegetarianism* (2005). A drifter, he makes his living performing odd jobs on the sidewalks. For more on Ly Doi, see "Introduction to Ly Doi and Bui Chat" in appendices.

Drilling and Cutting Concrete

must...
I will wipe out all of you [those who drill and cut concrete—you all] from the
bases of walls
I will wipe out mankind and animals
I will wipe out birds and fish
I will make the wicked wobble and fall
and exterminate mankind [as well as those who drill and cut concrete] from the
face of the earth...

must...
I will raise my arm and strike the traitors [and snitches]
and all the Viet settlers
I will exterminate from this place [including alley 47] all the adjacent settlers
who are left behind
and obliterate the names of sanctioned publishers
I will exterrminate those who climb to the roofs to beg for aids
I will exterminate those who crawl into the ground to search for a beautiful
grave [or a quiet tomb, same difference]

keep silent in my presence: Doi Ly—one who drills and cuts concrete...

and remember, I will use a lamp to search all over the Viet realm
I will punish the men,
I will insult the women
and abuse the homosexuals
those who are nonchalant like wine above dregs
they reassure themselves: since Doi Ly doesn't dispense benefits, he will not
unleash harms...
they are mistaken, in a totalitarian country
their properties will be stolen or destroyed,
their houses wrecked,
they build homes, but cannot live in them,
they grow grapes [or rice, same difference], but cannot drink the wine...

it's near, the day of Doi Ly
the day of heart-rending screams echoing
the day of wrath
the day of despair
the day of afflictions
the day of extermination & destruction

dark & blurry day
overcast & gloomy day
the day of devouring fire...

hey, all you shameless people, gather, gather together
before you will be scattered
like rice husks blown away by the winds in a day
and look at the phone numbers on advertisements for drilling and cutting
concrete
on the walls surrounding you all
that even earthquakes, or I (who can exterminate everything) cannot destroy...

      Note: This piece was composed when the Viet realm was experiencing earthquakes and volcanoes [8/2005], after 3,200 years. And when a volume of poetry [without this poem] is about to come out.

from Seven Spider Improvisations

doi ly spider performs a miracle walking on water

then doi immediately made his disciples get on a boat to cross the river, while doi begged money and capital from the crowd, and ascended a mountain to pray for a poetic inspiration, poetic inspiration and topic did not come, doi stayed there alone— like a grasping idiot... and already the literary boat was several arms-length from shore, beat back by the waves, all evening long and what's left of the night, until nearly cockcrow, doi finally stepped onto the dark surface of the water intending to cross the river, but the literary disciples saw and mistook him for an imposter and panicked, doi made a sign for them to calm down and called each disciple to abandon the boat to cross the river, one then two, then three, then countless others all entered the water... the situation occurred in an instant and no one saw it, but the disciples who were doubtful and without faith started to sink, doi pulled each one up and rubbed imaginary ointment on them, they thought of reaching the shore, of belonging to the group and having people pamper them... then the shore arrived, doi stood watching the familiar disciples with teary eyes, thanks to a miracle, for each one who made it to shore countless sank to the bottom, even those who did not doubt and were full of faith... all the surviving disciples were in shock, terrified, haughty then kowtowing: doi spider was truly an impostor—pretending to be a poem.

what defiles doi?

shortly after the crossing the river incident, doi summoned his remaining disciples and asked them: what defiles us, then [to set himself straight] answered: it's not what goes in but out of the mouth, the mouth is fouler than any other hole on your body and mine also! these things [phrases, strings of words...] are fouling me then you and I don't know what to do to make myself even more foul and continue... then the disciples approached and took turns answering: do you know, doi, those words can make the old-fashioned ungrammatical and lament to god; the wise guys of language grumble and scream about the absence of beauty, though the nosey and analytical fancy themselves useful... doi spider replied: among many disciples only a few can become trees and bear fruits, the rest are corpses at the river's bottom, the rest are blind and deceived, they lead each other and roll to wherever, it doesn't matter, how can I stop them... still uncomprehending, the disciples asked: so where can we roll to now... doi turned away from them: scram to wherever, I could care less, you idiotic and defiled, hanging out with you all, there's a risk that my mouth will freshen and my soul will become pure.

Society 3

Footnote for the Bodhisattva at Su Thai Temple:

Today a story appeared in the City Police newspaper about some deputy minister who habitually bought sexual favors [and dispositions] from children and was condemned to death, and here we have a matter worthy of attention that happened on the execution ground:

Since the guy was a master in wheeling and dealing [even selling out the people] he bought off the director/psychological [issues] advisor to the firing squad, to make these guys feel remorseful [as in their conscience shred into pieces] when they take out their guns to perform their duty. He also bought off the entire firing squad... the result: the hail of bullets only hit a soft [but tasty] spot and even the coup de grace, an extremely rare occurance, only glanced his skin— blood spilling all over... he pretended to faint, then fainted for real, then was revived by a waiting crew of doctors with their equipments...

But it seemed that the sky had blue eyes and a red beak... gloating over his complicated ploys, he grinned constantly while lying in hospital to be treated for his [mediocre] light wound. Discharged, he officially laughed out loud in [abject] satisfaction, but because he was not paying attention he slipped on a banana peel, fell and hit his head on a pebble that a little girl he had bought sex from had left behind after a [gay] game of tic tac toe. This time, with no [militant] crew of [dignified] doctors waiting nearby, he had to close his eyes and wait for [chilly] death but still he grinned [in gassy] in satisfaction because he had managed to escape his execution. Suddenly from afar echoed the voice of Mrs. Six living in a working class ghetto [someone who had nothing to do with him]:

If you must be reincarnated as a dog then be a German shepherd, a daschund or some Japanese breed... don't be a Vietnamese dog, you'll eat shit all day, are struck by people and even run the risk of being strung up by the neck and converted into 9 dogmeat dishes.

This entire poetic tale according to Mrs. Six is a type of third-rate sentimental film mixed with bits of fucking, ready to be rented at New Mountain [high spirit] market and shown nonstop at Su Thai temple.

THE BENEFITS OF POETRY

Poetry and Physical Beauty

Poetry is a great form of exercise. When you write poetry, it means that your muscles are active, your energy spent, your body becomes flexible, your figure slim and firm. You only need to write poetry two to three times a week, this practice is the best replacement for all other forms of daily exercises.

Writing poetry is also an excellent way to "tighten" the second circle, harden the third and invigorate the first. The stomach, buttocks and chest muscles are very active when you write poetry. According to a recent Chinese study, writing poetry combined with dancing to gentle rhythms such as Waltz, Tango and Swing.... will burn up a fair amount of calories, increase your height and juice up your sex drive...

A person who practices poetry regularly is also one with an elegant, classy appearance; and, of course, not without allure and attractiveness.

Poetry and Health

Poetry doesn't just bring a healthy body, a slim shape but can also help you to resist and prevent many illnesses. After many stressful working hours, exhausting, you can let yourself go with the lively, transforming constructions of a Rubai, a Sonnet, a Haiku, a Sung Dynasty styled poem, a 6/8, a free verse, a post-modernism... all your tensions and stresses will be shooed away quickly.

According to researches and investigations from America, someone who practices poetry can eliminate up to 70% of illnesses such as: insomnia, obesity, arthritis, depression, migraines and even diabetes. As your body is allowed to move rhythmically to the constructions and flows of words... your blood can circulate, your nervous system can unwind.

Once you've become an expert poet, you will have gained much experiences to be someone with the skills to socialize, make long-term plans and be especially confident. These benefits will help you greatly in life, work and play.

Poetry and Romance

Writing poetry with all your passion is definitely an activity to help you increase your human potential for being sensitive and romantic. As you succeed in feeling a poem, chasing after its inner movements, you become more sensitive. As with nearly everyone, we all want to become more attractive to a lover or a spouse. Nothing else will give you so many opportunities to trigger emotions, increase your attractiveness to a stranger of the opposite sex without saying a word, or do anything but spend a few minutes reading a poem together.

Poetry and Social Organization

Of course, unfortunately, writing poetry is also one of the causes of regrettable misunderstandings that can destroy your social contentment, and subvert society. The main cause is that poetry is still an oddity to many people, and on top of that there is a lack of positive knowledge of this mode of social communication among those in leadership positions all over the world.

In Vietnam, writing poetry is also spreading widely, relatively speaking. You can catch people writing poetry in many places, in the offices of the national assembly, parks, next to a lake and in locales where people gather to eat and use prostitutes. From early morning until dusk, late night and beyond. From preschool, youth, middle-age to even old age, everyone enjoys practicing poetry. A destination for those who want to participate, exchange, explore and research news about poetry in Vietnam: the various types of literature and art journals.

Poetry and Advice

Let's all practice poetry not only out of enjoyment but also because of the many advantages and attitudes that poetry can bring.

BUI CHAT is the pen name of Bui Quang Vien. Born in 1979 in Bien Hoa, he lives in Ho Chi Minh City. A member of the Open Mouth group, Bui Chat has been published on webzines and in group samizdats such as *Six-Sided Circle* (2002) and *Open Mouth* (2002), and in his own samizdat, *Deesturbances Tooday* (2003). In 2011, Bui Chat was awarded the International Publishers Association's Freedom to Publish Prize "for his exemplary courage in upholding freedom to publish." For more on Bui Chat, see "Introduction to Ly Doi and Bui Chat" in appendices.

Kurrent State

nothin kan seize me from da hands
a look doesn't korrespond to da fi fingers
between da rite and left eyes
not da blue runny nose
dis world kannot squeeze me
old images alter me same as new
attittude on toilet skuattin to drop one thing into water
don't want to sneeze with da crowd
I am da pregnancy inside da belly of da gurl I luv

Upside Down Pole

All ways upside down
spread
da broom
some eyes writhin
look sideways
leenin against wall I want feet to be head
I sing
about shorts coiled springs being sic in bed
da faulty sentiment of missin stuff
& apathy
dis bleek room has been ma breath?
I must lic da uneveness around stuff
den flip
upside down
all ways
how to do all things
spread nite and day I seduce da wall
hornily flap
da lips
never stepped ouside my shorts face

Stab Skin

I thro spit onto da wall
I luv women who are sewer rats
I see you wearing 33 cent panties bought on da sidewalk
books don't make me better each Sunday
I see myself flyin in da sky
I torture myself three meals a day
I stab skin
I shout for words
I organize wars
I chant namyo to God
I lash ma tomb teeth in da mornin
I stab skin
I reform da uterus
I a divorce paper

Late Floing Wind

H a master masterbaitin Writes
Poetry cannot be rushed life's philled
with dismal priks Give up
accrueing dreams Fleas
durin time of turmoil Thinkin of da flesh plot I
a person wit an itchin eye
A gatherin herd of water logged responses*
Surrouns me like trash
Perhaps a feemale foot deep inside da earth
with two hollow breasts
I shout an expanse
Everythin's blu
Inside da words
From a wandrin look sedoocin da whorizon
I orient ma head
I must keep silent even if onlee in one ear
By throin back da whorries
As I don't cease growin & goin
Flyin towards somewhe known for a late flowin wind clock

Translator's note:
*water logged responses: from the poetry of Tran Tien Dung

Ing Rhymes

I want to cry like I want to vomit
on the street
crystal sunlight
I call my own name to soothe my longing
thanh tam tuyen
[o crap, I meant bui chat!]
evening a star breaks against a church bell
boing! boing!
I need a secret place to kneel
for a little one whose soul
fears viscious dog
a starving brown dog
barks
gaw! gaw!

I want to die like I want to sleep
although I'm standing on a river bank
the deep dark water is restless
I scream my own name to slake my rage
bui chet! bui chet!
night falls onto a sinful whispering realm
O child wearing a red kerchief
hey there wolf
a wandering sort of wolf
though very upright

I crave suicide
an eternal sort of murderer
I scream my own name in distress
buoi chet! buoi chet! bu u u o o i i i che e e t t t!
strangle myself into collapsing
so I could be resurrected

today my wife suddenly menstruates...

[this poem is a parody of Thanh Tam Tuyen's very famous 1956 poem,
"Resurrection." Twenty of 31 lines are identical with the original.]

for the spirit. for the body. for living or five reasons why you should choose vietnamese poetry

an advertisement to assist ly doi at the vietnamese poetry booth, at the all-world poetry fair (planned for 2012)

trust
it's a product that has endured for a thousand years

reliance
it has been proven by science to be a food with many nutritional benefits

certified
it has been granted the certifications ISO 9001: 2000, ISO 14001, GMP & HACCP

guaranteed
no cholesterol, no chemical preservatives, no artificial colorings

a necessity for an active life
because vietnamese poetry is a nutritious food:
- provides instant energy for the body
- increases the body's immunity & spiritual strength
- contributes to a speedy recovery of your health
- improves memory & mental power
- helps to alleviate psychic tension
- improves young mothers' abilities to breast feed
- is good for your blood thanks to its ability to absorb and use iron

note: this product is not a medicine, and should not be substituted for medicines

LYNH BACARDI's real name is Pham Thi Thuy Linh. She was born in 1981 in Ho Chi Minh City, where she still lives. A 5th grade drop out, she has worked as an itinerant vendor of cakes, duck embryos, newspapers and lottery tickets, and is now a typist and a translator of self-help books. She has published poems and stories in several leading Vietnamese literary journals and webzines. Translated into English, her works have appeared in *Tinfish* and *Nha Magazine*. In an interview, she explains that her pen name is derived from **Linh Yêu** [loves] **Nh**iên [the name of her boyfriend, poet Than Nhien], a love that's as fierce as Bacardi rum. In an interview, she comments about her use of blunt and aggressive language: "I'm not trying to shock by deliberately using such language, but the subject matters and materials I've chosen to bring into poetry are often seen as dismal, dark and belonging to the depths of society. Things that, before, people didn't dare to bring into poetry. So I would contradict myself if I used beautiful and elegant words."

Shrink & Stretch

today waking up speaking like an opportunistic death rim. I cry buzzingly
a scrawny milk cow. missing the last grasping chance. mother sits counting
money inside a jar brimming with black water. a hot line for polluted spirits.
outside all living things are in mourning clothes and trampling on each other
to reach heaven. I uncouth a building built with virginal blood. feigning an
orgasmic moan. sunlight high above weeping inundating the streets. men
who become bloodless when overburdened. the obese rain flows hotly. I'm
pregnant with coins reeking a burning smell. a mother selling her flow keeping
the cultural flow for her brood. needle marks wilting along with each vein.
numbly I chew the cheery invoice. the ulcerated mouth teaches civilization to its
children. I give birth to well-off swindlers. a tiny body running after a beer can
recklessly tilting. drooling at leftover food inside the eyes. bad nerves jamming
the buddha's miracles. a shivering fairy guffawing up a pack of lice. today all
ideas upset the stomach. a look loaded with the code of one who defecates
often. hey little girl laughing savagely a prurient pain. let's wear the voice of
the opportunistic death rim. I carry your shadow into a coffin bought with a
bitter tongue. headstrong words trading blows with each other. stepping on
red coals I walk spellbound. budding pubic hairs dying of old age. at midnight
laughs and cries grind down the city. the malnourished timid whirlwind. I sold
my ass seven times the first time. pay back with a bout of love making without
joy. woke up the next morning with a blood-smeared death rim. virginal blood
more precious than living blood. a mother laughing baring her teeth inside a jar
brimming with black water. I drape my skirt over lumpy heads encrusted with
woven spider shit. now my male member festers.

10/03

Badmouthing Oneself

rubbing salt on a wound not yet encrusted. choking the overflowing source of
piety. how to freeze frame perfection. I banish all erupting emotions. the ladle
scornfully splatter a smooth face. sterility drifts inside consciousness. goose
flesh kindling disease. I howl into the void. breed wild dogs inside the body. the
bra suddenly dries up binding each vertebrae. the generational divide rotted
and buried in earth. nakedly glowering demanding to be worshipped. male
members lined up permanently risen. I 5 feet 5 after recovering my dignity.
an intellectual hawking the equivalent of a rotten egg. two rubber sacks at face
value. I stand on my head wearing a pair of three-legged pants. the microphone
from the rally sprouting bristles. I tear the third pant leg. in need of a few holes
to penetrate tonight. will be brainy tomorrow. the bible bleeding black blood
at the head of the bed. the gospel hits the road. I rejuvenate the brain with a
coat of status paint bought from the open-air market. asskicking high class. will
turn into a child this evening. bound by the word "far" weighing down the neck
while being carried by "mother." greedy eyes a mouthful of milk. two knees
suddenly numb on the barbed wires. praying hoping to give birth to a flock
of suns. like to illuminate distances with insolent laughter. I crave the smell
of piss from the rat hole neighborhood. roaming around carrying a flat face.
bad-mouth the past betray the present. the cock on the church's roof clucks.
I shift sex. put hands together for the end of the day's prayer. tonight I gobble
once more the sacrament. look for a new brand tomorrow – surely people are
disgusted.

10/03

APPENDIX

What's New in Vietnamese Poetry

A talk given by Linh Dinh at Naropa University, Boulder, Colorado,
on July 20, 2005

transcribed by Laura Wright

I'd like to give you a background on Vietnamese poetry, the context in which
this kind of poetry is written. The thing about Vietnam is that the oral tradition
was very much alive until fairly recently. And it's still alive. I would say that
most Vietnamese over 40 know at least a dozen of these folk poems. I've
translated a lot of these folk poems because I'm very drawn to them; they are
very earthy, they can be very raunchy, and they deal with everything, all aspects
of life. One thing I don't like about the folk poems is the rhythm. It's a popular
form and it's passed from mouth to mouth, and its music tends to be fairly
predictable, usually 6/8 form. This 6/8 form is fine in itself, it's just that when
you hear it so much it becomes part of how you hear language, and it permeates
every kind of writing in Vietnam. So the writers I'm most interested in who are
writing poems right now are the ones who slice up this rhythm. Consequently
a lot of them are not read by the general public. The public reads these poems
and they say they don't sound like poems, because they don't hear that rhythm.
Just to give you a taste of that rhythm I'm going to read three folk poems in the
original language. You can hear the sing-song rhythm.

> Gà tơ xào với mướp già.
> Vợ hai mươi mốt, chồng đã sáu mươi.
> Ra đường, chị giễu em cười.
> Rằng hai ông cháu kết đôi vợ chồng.
> Đêm nằm, tưởng cái gối bông,
> Giật mình gối phải râu chồng nằm bên.
> Sụt sùi tủi phận hôn duyên,
> Oán cha, trách mẹ tham tiền bán con.

Young hen stir-fried with old loofah.
Wife twenty one, husband sixty.
On the streets, women joke, girls giggle.
Granddad, granddaughter a married pair.
At night, a cotton-stuffed pillow I'm hugging
Turns out to be my bearded husband.
Sniffling, I feel sorry for myself, curse my fate,
Curse my greedy parents who sold their daughter.

Đôi ta như thể con tằm,
Cùng ăn một lá, cùng nằm một nong.

The two of us are like a pair of silkworms,
Eating the same leave, lying in the same basket.

Văn chương chữ nghĩa bề bề,
Thần lồn ám ảnh cũng mê mẩn người.

Inundated with books, he is
Still haunted by the vagina.

That sense of humor — actually they go farther than what you find in the official poetry. There are many examples of that. These are things people tell each other as they're drinking, talking, joking around.

[…]

Khe Iem lives in Los Angeles and was a Domino's Pizza delivery man. I'm giving you these details because this is how—I love these guys because of the fact that they go on, in spite of everything. Anyway, he managed to start a poetry journal that up 'til two years ago he was still running. Khe Iem is interesting to me also because he started out such an interesting poet and editor and somewhere along the way I think he just went wrong because he got really involved with the New Formalists. He became infected with this sort of American disease, it's not something that was happening in Vietnam. He became so militant about the New Formalism that he started translating a bunch of these people, the least interesting American poetry, and lecturing people about it constantly. So at some point I thought, wow, this is very dangerous, because he is in charge of the poetry magazine most Vietnamese poets were reading, and the ones in Vietnam didn't know what was really happening here. So for this guy to keep going on about the New Formalist movement sort of distorted what was happening here. And people inside Vietnam would think that's really what's happenin' here, maybe that's the only thing happening here. So at one point I came out and in an interview I just said, listen, this is nonsense. Because so much is happening, there are so many strains here and I'm sorry but I don't know why Khe Iem is doing this.

[…]

When I returned to Vietnam in '99, most of the poets I met were not that interesting because they were sort of intimidated from writing anything that might get them in trouble. Nguyen Quoc Chanh stood out because of his fearlessness. He would say anything in any context. You'd find some people would be very guarded in any kind of public situation, including a cafe, they wouldn't say certain things; but Chanh was just constantly talking. Even his friends were worried about him, saying maybe you shouldn't be so open, you don't know who's at the table.

In the early '90s there was a brief moment when people were able to publish more risqué material and Chanh's first book of poems came out of that time. It was greeted with a lot of hostility in the newspapers, which are government controlled. The book is called *Night of the Rising Sun*, and one review called Chanh's book "a cemetery of the spirit and of the body. There's nothing left for a person to look for or to lean on. This book can only lead man towards madness, irresponsibility, obliviousness towards the present, humans and objects. The lofty and the abject, the real and the fake, right and wrong, virtues and cruelties are here mixed together in a slimy, disgusting blob" Another review stated that this writer will end up burnt by the fire that he is messing with.

[…]

Chanh talks about himself: "I was born in a dull place, Bac Lieu, into a dull family, went to dull schools not worth mentioning, with dull teachers not worth mentioning. And now, although I live in the brilliant and chaotic city, Saigon, I have no alternative but to become a dull person. And I have to take anti-stress pills every day."

[…]

Lynh Bacardi is sort of influenced by Chanh, but she has her own thing going. I first encountered her poems online and I was amazed by the energy, the weirdness of these poems. About a month ago she had this to say in an interview. It echoes what Chanh was saying and this is a general sentiment: "I studied many things I did not want to study, memorized many things I did not want to memorize; did not get to study things I wanted to know more about. I have not been out of the country. Walking in circles, I look down then up. Thanks to the internet, the mouth of the well has become wider although the bottom is still narrow." There's a Vietnamese proverb about a frog sitting on the bottom of a well who thinks that's the whole universe. She's referring to that.

[…]

Mien Dang was born in Da Nang in 1974, came to the U.S. in 1989, and now lives in Tampa, where she works as a manicurist. It's interesting how these people are spread out around the world but they stay together through the internet and their love of poetry. Mien Dang is also partially deaf. She studies with monks, two Burmese monks, but her poems seem, I don't know, not very serene. That's what I like about her, the
fact that she has a different side of her.

[…]

Question: It seems like a connecting factor for a lot of these poets is the internet and a love of poetry. Do you know of any sort of community, whether online or in print that reaches into other Southeast Asian languages or immigrant populations? Particularly countries like the Philippines that have had a lot of American influence also, where English is a language that's commonly used. Are there any sort of dialects that you know of?

Linh Dinh: I don't know. I can talk more about the Vietnamese websites, the particulars of these websites. One website updates every day, so the energy is always there. People look forward to reading it. I read it in the morning, because they update it in the morning, but in Vietnam that would be at night. So people would turn to it like a newspaper. Every day there are new translations and new poetry. I don't know of any American website that does that. I think it's very exciting. The problem is how to maintain quality, usually you have three or four new pieces a day, so some days it's not so great. Actually I think it influences how people are writing too, because they can respond to each other's poems and see it online — instead of your typical journal where you wait six months or a year to see it.

Q: I was struck by the, for lack of a better term, image-based, almost surrealist threads that ran through a lot of the poems that you read. I was wondering if you could talk about influences in or for Vietnamese poetry to get to that point.

L D: I'm glad you asked that because it's very important to point that out — why there's so much surrealism. First off, they were allowed to be translated. The surrealists were communists so there was no problem translating them, although their poetics has nothing to do with socialist realism, that was more the official line. So their books were available. Another book that was very influential was *A Hundred Years of Solitude*, because Marquez was also a communist. So the censors would say, this guy's a communist so this is OK. Really the work is not communist writing. Also, surrealism is a way to talk indirectly and not get in trouble. Really these censors are not that bright. They read stuff like this and don't know what the hell's going on. But there's a danger in that too, you can get too convoluted and too weird. I think the government also encourages a kind of soft surrealism. Some of the official poets also write in a kind of vaguely surrealist style without any political or deeper connotations. One guy I like to ridicule all the time always brings ghosts into his poems, so he gives it a 'mystical' kind of feel but it's really nonsense. In one poem the ghost could be a cow—all these things are talking and floating around... And he's the official poet, or one of them.

Q (Michael Davidson): The previous questioner asked the question I wanted to ask, which is something about predecessors. You started out by talking about this folk tradition, but I'm wondering about a classical tradition which all of the writers would be directly responding to?

L D: The so-called national poem is 3,400 lines or something, it's the story of a prostitute. A lot of people have problems with this poem because of its values, like sacrifice and resignation, so this poem has been debated on forever. But that's the poem that is always held up as the Vietnamese masterpiece. Another problem I have with it is that its plot was borrowed from a Chinese text. I think people keep returning to this poem because of its language, it's fresh. It was written [by Nguyen Du] in 1817, but the Vietnamese in it is very rich and very beautiful. So the language is great, the story is not so great—it's a woman who sacrificed herself to save her father. A lot of people have pointed out— why do we want to have a poem about a prostitute be our national poem? The Vietnamese language now is written in the alphabet, this poem is written in the native script, which is no longer in use; hardly anyone knows it anymore. Another poet who has a lot of influence is Ho Xuan Huong. She wrote a lot of raunchy poems. John Balaban translates some of these poems. I have a problem with John's versions because on the cover he has a bare-breasted woman next to a gong or something, and I think, *come on*. But it's more complex than that, you could build her up as a woman ahead of her time—she was early 19th century, late 18th century—you could build her up as a bold, sexually aggressive woman. But most of those poems were probably not written by her. I would say none of them were written by her, because the only book that was compiled of this body of poetry, the only surviving book is a century later. During that gap so many texts... One book might have 70 poems, another book might have 50, another book might have 40, and there are all these arguments about which ones are authentic. I think they belong more properly to the folk tradition. So we should talk about the Ho Xuan Huong tradition, rather than— what I'm trying to say is, it's fine that the peasants liked the idea of a sexually aggressive and dirty-talking woman, it's great. The folk poems are like that anyway. But many of these poems are probably written by men too, and what do you make of that?

These are held up as the two—Truyen Kieu is the first one and then Ho Xuang Huong—they are like the Whitman and the Dickinson of Vietnam.

Q: I was wondering about the relationship between Vietnamese culture and sexuality – a lot of the poems are dealing pretty intensely with sexuality. I was wondering if it was due possibly to some sexual repression in the past or whether its a pretty free culture in terms of sexual expression?

L D: I think with the material on the web, since there are no censors, it's gotten to be very aggressively sexual, by men and by women. One new group of poets, these guys are in their mid-twenties, call themselves Mo Mieng which means 'open mouth.' They are getting a lot of attention now, they are the most sexual people, I think they're influenced by rap music. When I first encountered the open mouth guys I like it, because I liked the defiance in their work. In Vietnam people live with their parents for too long, because of economics or tradition; some people never leave their parents. The parents are such an oppressive presence in the Vietnamese psyche. So when I encountered these very young guys in their early twenties writing very aggressively, writing kind of belligerent poems, I applauded. I know these kids. Then at a certain point I realized something is not quite right, the rap thing and the misogyny in there is something I cringe at. But what can I do? I almost regret some of the statements I've made in interviews endorsing these people. But I endorse also the female writers who write very aggressively. I think it's a trend right now. They're basically punks, these kids are punks, male and female. There's room for that for now. It's good because it's overthrowing the elders, like saying fuck you, get out of my face.

[...]

Q: Are there any debates concerning language between the people who are not in Vietnam and the writers still working in Vietnam? For instance with other languages, especially Spanish, writers who are abroad are sometimes criticized by writers who stay in Mexico because they think the language has been to some degree corrupted and they're not speaking 'pure' Spanish anymore and not writing it and they're maybe too open to outside influences. So I was wondering if there was any kind of debate between the writers in Vietnam and the writers abroad?

L D: What I find most interesting is some of the most corrupted writers are in Vietnam. They are more enthralled by English, so they tend to throw in English more. When I write in Vietnamese I never use English, so I'm purer than them. They'll throw in English words all over the place, some of them that is, not all of them, because they think it's cool. I don't need to do that. I think there's also a tension, the ones in Vietnam look at the ones from the outside with a kind of— most of us get along pretty well, but I'm sure some of them probably resent the fact that we are outside, for many reasons. They would like to dismiss us as not relevant. Some of them who come here are treated very well by the Vietnamese community, and then they go back and they never mention who they met, they just dismiss us, they block us out. I think some of that is pure cowardice because they don't want to get in trouble with the government. There are a number of people who don't acknowledge Vietnamese writing overseas at all and I think most of that has to do with politics, but some of that could be just personal. For whatever reason they don't want to acknowledge us. I was talking to a man recently from Hanoi who said some people told him that what I write is not even poetry because it sounds so flat. Maybe that's the critique, my Vietnamese sounds so odd to some of these people's ears. Isn't that the whole purpose of it? We've got the pure stuff, let's mix it up, let's pollute it up.

Q: You were talking about the strong oral tradition until recently of the folk poem and how that's beginning to disappear. I was wondering what accounts for that disappearance?

L D: Because most people were illiterate until a century ago. And with improved literacy there was no need to store everything in the oral tradition. But it lingers on, even after people became literate it kept going: in slogans, in advertising, that rhythm persists.

Linh Dinh interviews Phan Nhien Hao

Linh Dinh: In April of 1975, you were only 5 years old. You stayed in Vietnam until 1991, then immigrated to the U.S. Growing up in a Socialist environment, what did you read? How did these writers influence your thoughts and poetics?

Phan Nhien Hao: It's true that in April of 1975, I was still very little. But I believe that the most important factors in shaping one's character are the things one learns in the first years of childhood. April of 1975 also affected my family in a tragic way, and I think this has determined my consciousness, although, like all children in South Vietnam after 1975, I grew up with a Socialist education. To overcome the political difficulties of my family background, I tried to be an excellent student throughout my elementary and secondary schools. I was one of the best literature students in the entire country. This means I had to memorize a lot of Socialist writing to compete in the best student contests. Thanks to this, I was admitted directly into the Teachers' College, and didn't have to join the military to fullfil my "international duties" in Cambodia. Although I had to study this literature to compete in the contests, I had from the beginning seen it as mechanical and tedious. Fortunately, my family managed to keep a library of books translated before 1975. I still remember hiding under the table at ten-years-old to read books that my uncle deemed inappropriate for my age. This library had truly contributed to the development of my literary consciousness. During my college years in Saigon, I also found many books published before 1975 to read. I don't think my studying Socialist literature has really affected my thoughts in any substantial way, because I was always secretly resisting it even as I was forced to study it, because my family background had taught me who I really was. And because I was living in the South, where there were still many books published before 1975.

LD: Can you speak about the influence of surrealism in your poetry?

PNH: I think the influence of surrealism has become too vast and deep in 20th century arts. Nowadays you can find traces of surrealism in nearly all modern and postmodern works. To me, surrealism is only the means to see beyond the surface of things, and, more importantly, it's a method to make associations in poetry. Surrealist associations allow the poet to place next to each other images that do not seem to go together in ordinary life, it allows the imagination to widen, and from there to create a richer reality. Another important element in surrealism is automatic writing, which I think is a very useful poetic device. This creates surprises in poetry, and frees it from the narrative task. And yet, I still try to build each poem as an integrated whole, linked by a unity of emotion, within the very ambiguity and unexpected shifts of the images. I think surrealism has become an element in contemporary poetry, so it's only natural that there are traces of surrealism in my poetry.

LD: You have a degree in American literature from UCLA. Encountering American literature for the first time, what were your reactions? What do you see as the differences between American and Vietnamese literatures?

PNH: In Vietnam, even before 1975, far fewer American writers were translated and introduced to Vietnamese readers than French writers. After 1975, only a handful of "progressive" American writers were translated. That's why, before coming to the US, I thought American literature was similar to European literature. My first reaction to American literature was disappointment. American literature seemed too monotonous, it wasn't a type of literature imbued with philosophy, with lots of experimentations, like contemporary French literature. But then I understood that the direct, non fussy quality of American literature is a feature that has been consciously and systematically built by American writers. It's an effort to create a distinct American literature, suitable to a consumer society and a pragmatic culture, with that American emphasis on results. My experience of American literature went hand in hand with my growing understanding of American culture and assimilation into American life, and not only something I learnt at school. That's why I think it would be hard for people living in Vietnam, where the influence of French culture is still very strong, to see the beauty of American literature. But I believe that an investigation into American literature would greatly benefit Vietnamese writers. It would make them less prone to heavy philosophizing, and improve their sense of humor. I just want to emphasize that, more than any other country, the U.S. is a multi-cultural society. And that's also true of American literature. The generalizations I've made about American literature are only its most salient features, and not all the particulars of American literature. In a free place like America, writers certainly do not have to compose in a single fashion.

LD: How has being in exile affected your poetry?

PNH: I feel lucky to have arrived in the U.S. at an age young enough to continue my education, but not too young that I only had a superficial knowledge of Vietnam. That's why I can compare, and detect the differences between the two cultures and literatures. Life is lonely here, but people do have an opportunity to do whatever they want, and say whatever they think, without someone to harass them. People don't starve to death here. And I don't think a poet can ask for more. The other issues are personal. The somewhat isolated life of an immigrant here has allowed me to turn inward more, and for my thinking to mature more. My knowledge of American literature and culture makes me want to write more directly and more vigorously. Life has its problems everywhere, but this is the exile life I have chosen, and I will never regret having made that decision.

[from a longer interview published in the Australia-based Vietnamese language journal, VIET, No. 8 (2001). This English translation first appeared in *Night, Fish and Charlie Parker: the poetry of Phan Nhien Hao* (Tupelo 2006)]

Introducing Ly Doi and Bui Chat

Officially known as Ho Chi Minh City, Saigon is a mess. Only 300 years old, it is way overpopulated, its congestion broken up only by sewer-like rivers and creeks. Hung-over from decades of wars and revolutions, it's a cocktail of unpredictable sights, noises and smells, and has a raw, exasperating energy. There is nothing refi ned about Saigon. It'll hug you tight, molesting you, and won't let go until you either strangle or marry it.

Scooters, cyclos, careening vans, overloaded trucks, pushcarts and beggars on dollies swarm its streets from 5 in the morning until 2 at night. Its architecture is a moldy French/Vietnamese hybrid left over from Colonial times, mixed with no-nonsense box-like buildings from the 60's and 70's, American style, and slick new skyscrapers downtown. Soviet statuary mars its rare parks. Sly, crass, incoherent and frankly infatuated with all things foreign, Saigon mimics everyone and proclaims itself an original.

I met Ly Doi and Bui Chat in Saigon in July of 2001 at a party at poet Tran Tien Dung's house. They had just graduated from the university and not yet published. I didn't know them then. At the party, I recognized translator Cu An Hung and poets Nguyen Dat, Phan Ba Tho and Nguyen Quoc Chanh. All of us sat on straw mats on the floor, drank, ate and shot the shit for hours. Born in 1957, Chanh was (and is) the most respected underground poet in Saigon. Despised by the establishment, his poetry is described by one critic as "a cemetery of the spirit and the body." Though absent from offi cial journals and anthologies, Chanh is an inspiring presence to his peers, and provides a model for younger poets like Ly Doi and Bui Chat. More or less banned from publishing, Chanh has to contend himself with appearing on webzines and samizdats.

I'd bet that Ly Doi and Bui Chat are also inspired by a poet from the previous generation, Bui Giang, the lost soul of Saigon. Not for his style, which was rather traditional, but for his raving, whoring madness, his lust for experience, his love of learning, his outcast status and his dedication to poetry. Bui Giang translated Camus, Gide, Heidegger and René Char, among others. He wrote about Sartre, Confucius, Lao Tzu and Gandhi. By his own admission, he started to become "brilliantly mad" in 1969. After 1975, he slept in a squalid shack next to a turbid pond.

Defiant and reckless, Bui Chat and Ly Doi revel in their outcast status. They drift from place to place, do odd jobs to make money, gather at sidewalk cafes to drink and talk with other poets. With Nguyen Quan and Khuc Dzuy they form a small group calling themselves Mo Mieng, or "Open Your Mouth." Yes, sometimes they suck or say stupid things—who doesn't—but when they're on their game, they can also be brilliantly mad.

Some applaud them as a turning point in Vietnamese poetry. Others sneer that they're all attitude and no substance. The Goethe Institute in Hanoi was intrigued enough to invite them to read in June of 2005, only to have to cancel the event at the last minute under pressure from Vietnamese authorities. The government had previously jailed Ly Doi and Bui Chat in 2003 for 2 days for passing out
flyers at another cancelled reading.

Among the Vietnamese government's rationalizations for this latest cancellation, as reported by the BBC: "[T]he poetry group Mo Mieng is not serious, with works that are downright obscene." Read on and judge for yourself.

[published in *CALQUE*, no. 3, 2007]

About the Editor/Translator

LINH DINH was born in Saigon, Vietnam in 1963, came to the US in 1975, and has also lived in Italy and England. He is the author of two collections of stories, *Fake House* (Seven Stories 2000) and *Blood and Soap* (Seven Stories 2004), five books of poems, *All Around What Empties Out* (Tinfish 2003), *American Tatts* (Chax 2005), *Borderless Bodies* (Factory School 2006), *Jam Alerts* (Chax 2007), and *Some Kind of Cheese Orgy* (Chax 2009), and a novel about Vietnam, *Love Like Hate* (Seven Stories 2010). His work has been anthologized in *Best American Poetry 2000, 2004* and *2007*, *Great American Prose Poems from Poe to the Present* and *Norton's Postmodern American Poetry* (second edition), among other publications. He is also the editor of the anthologies *Night, Again: Contemporary Fiction from Vietnam* (Seven Stories 1996), and translator of *Night, Fish and Charlie Parker, the poetry of Phan Nhien Hao* (Tupelo 2006). His current project is a blog of photos and political essays, *State of the Union,* which will result in a book, *Postcards from the End of America*. Dinh has also published widely in Vietnamese.

About Chax Press

Chax Press is a 501(c)(3) nonprofit organization, founded in 1984, and has published more than 140 books, including fine art and trade editions of literature and book arts works.

For more information, please see our web site at http://chax.org

Chax Press is supported by individual contributions, and by the Tucson Pima Art Council and the Arizona Commision on the Arts, with funds from the State of Arizona and the National Endowment for the Arts. Particular thanks to this book go to the 117 individual donors to our 2013 Kickstarter campaign, of which this book is the fourth (of four) publication to be issued.

 TUCSON PIMA **A R T S** **C O U N C I L**

Arizona Commission on the Arts

N A T I O N A L ENDOWMENT FOR THE ARTS